Winners of the WH Smith Plays for Children Awards

Burning Everest
and
Mariza's Story

Introduction and questions by Alison Jenkins

Series editor: Lawrence Till

Heinemann Educational Publishers
Halley Court, Jordan Hill, Oxford OX2 8EJ
a division of Reed Educational & Professional Publishing Ltd
OXFORD MELBOURNE AUCKLAND
JOHANNESBURG BLANTYRE GABORONE
IBADAN PORTSMOUTH (NH) USA CHICAGO

The moral rights of the authors have been exercised

Burning Everest copyright © 1992 Adrian Flynn
Mariza's Story copyright © 1992 Michele Celeste

Introduction, notes and questions copyright © 1994 Alison Jenkins
Series Editor: Lawrence Till
All rights reserved

First published in 1994
First published in the *Heinemann Plays* series
08 07 06 05 04 03 02 01 00
15 14 13 12 11 10 9 8 7

A catalogue record for this book is available
from the British Library on request.
ISBN 0 435 23308 4

All rights whatsoever in these plays are strictly reserved. Requests to reproduce
either text in whole or in part should be addressed to the publishers. Application
for performance in any medium or for translation into any language should be
addressed to the author c/o the publishers.

Cover design by Keith Pointing

Original design by Jeffrey White Creative Associates; adapted by Jim Turner

Typeset by CentraCet Limited, Cambridge

Printed by Clays Ltd, St Ives plc

CONTENTS

Introduction   v

Burning Everest
List of Characters   x
The Play
  Act One   1
  Act Two   42

Mariza's Story
List of Characters   70
The Play
  Act One   71
  Act Two   108

Questions and Explorations
Burning Everest
1 Keeping Track: Act One   143
                       Act Two   145
2 Explorations: A Mallory's Expedition   147
                           B Hurt   148
                           C Character   149
                           D Stereotypes   149
                           E Daydreaming   149
Glossary   152

Mariza's Story

1	Keeping Track: Act One	154
	Act Two	156
2	Explorations: A Staging Mariza's Story	157
	B The Set	157
	C Brazilian Street Children	158
	D Character	159
	E Mothers	159

Glossary 161

INTRODUCTION

The WH Smith 'Plays for Children Award'

The WH Smith 'Plays for Children Award' 1992 attracted over eight hundred entries. The judging panel, which included the writer Adrian Mitchell, Susan Tully (Michelle in *EastEnders*) and *Blue Peter*'s Diane Louise Jordan were so impressed with *Burning Everest* and *Mariza's Story* that they awarded both first prize.

The plays

The two plays share a common theme: both concern children who, in different ways, have 'lost' their mothers. Many children, in Britain and across the world do not live in conventional two-parent families. All kinds of circumstances prevent them from doing so; divorce, death, poverty, illness are just some of the reasons for this.

In *Mariza's Story*, Mariza quite literally 'loses' her mum on a dark, lonely night on a road in a Brazilian city. In *Burning Everest*, Jim's separation is due to his mum's inability to continue looking after him, following the death of the grandmother who brought him up.

Burning Everest by Adrian Flynn

When Jim's mother finds she cannot continue to look after him he is sent to a caring foster family, the Wellands. Jim's own choice would be to stay with his mother and he finds it difficult to cope with her rejection of him. He has to start a new life in a new home and at a new school, there some teachers are extremely unfair and refuse to appreciate the difficulties he is having to face. Jim becomes so upset and angry that he alienates himself from everyone, even his best friend Stubby.

When life becomes too difficult to accept he escapes into his own fantasy world, and at times his obsession with George Mallory's ascent on Everest takes over his whole life, pushing aside reality. As his friend Stubby says, 'games are better than real life'.

The play asks all kinds of questions about the way children are treated by adults, about children's lack of control over their own lives, about our attitudes towards those with a physical disability or mental illness, and about how it can become easier to simply stereotype people rather than spending time getting to know what they're really like.

Mariza's Story by Michele Celeste

The circumstances that keep Mariza from her mother in *Mariza's Story* are quite different. In a harshly realistic portrayal of street life in Brazil, Michele Celeste shows us how young Mariza becomes separated from her mother and sister, and how bad luck and desperate poverty keep them apart.

Mariza, too young to read and write and even to remember where she's from, has to try to make a life for herself on the streets. She teams up with an old woman who, in a desperate state herself, exploits the young girl. Mariza then becomes part of Rambo's gang; a group of streetkids who stick together for some kind of protection and companionship.

But, whether with her friends or not, life is hard. The grinding poverty and very real danger of being murdered by the police in their effort to 'tidy up the streets', leaves no room for Mariza to experience a normal childhood. She has to grow up quickly in this brutal environment.

The play explores how Mariza manages to cope with her life on the streets without the guidance and security of a home life. Like so many other street children, Tania, her sister, does not survive.

The play also explores the desperation of Mariza's mother as she searches helplessly for her daughters. Poverty does not just destroy children.

Suggestions for follow-up work can be found at the end of the plays. The first section *Keeping Track* comprises straightforward questions on the text to help you consider what is happening in the play. These can be completed orally in class discussion or in note form, as you read through the play.

Suggestions for a more detailed look at some of the issues raised in the play follow in the *Explorations* section.

Alison Jenkins

Burning Everest

Adrian Flynn

List of Characters

Jim McLindon	Thirteen years old
Sharon McLindon	His mother. Late twenties
Mr and Mrs Welland	Jim's new foster parents. Thirties
Miranda Welland	Their daughter. Thirteen years old
Stubby Redshaw	A friend of Jim's with a prosthetic boot. Thirteen years old
Tony Simmons	Jim's social worker. Early twenties
Matt Davis	Fast Food takeaway owner. Thirties
Mr Bryant	The Headmaster of St Xavier's. Thirties
Mr Cooper and Mrs Pryme	Two teachers at St Xavier's
Peter	A pupil at St Xavier's

ACT ONE

Scene One

The stage is in darkness. There is a low wind that builds to a gale as the stage is suddenly revealed in as much white light as possible. There should be white or reflective drapes to produce a dazzling effect.

The wind abates slightly as Jim McLindon walks on. He is dressed in a faded T-shirt and torn jeans. He is aware of the wind and the cold but is more in awe of what he sees around him. He runs to the front of the stage and points behind him.

Jim   Chomolungma! That's it. There, you see? Chomolungma. The highest place on earth. Never been climbed; it's never been climbed. Chomolungma ... Oh, there is another name for it – Everest, Mount Everest, but it had a name long before the British came here. The Tibetans call it Goddess Mother of the World. Chomolungma. That's a name. That's a name for a mountain; for the mountain. She's beautiful – not 'beautiful' like a nice, sunny day in spring though. It's beauty like a drug; terrifying, taking you over, till your whole life is set on climbing her, being the first to reach the summit. You'd tear your lungs out; scramble and sweat over the frozen rock – you'd take your life in your hands and hang by a rope over a thousand feet of nothing, to stand on that peak – to be on top of the world. I should know. I've tried twice. Been beaten back by exhaustion, by the lack of air near the top. But this time I'll get there; I won't come down defeated.

For the first time Jim notices the cold and stamps to get warm.

Couldn't have had a worse day to set up base camp

though; still twelve miles from the foot of the mountain. But what does the cold matter? Pitching tents, breaking open the crates and testing the oxygen equipment's going to keep us busy here. We'll soon warm up.

Jim looks for a good spot to pitch a tent. He looks out to the audience, speaking from the front of the stage.

I'm George by the way.

He calls out off stage.

Come on Irvine, come on Odell; can't you make those porters get a shift on? We don't want to lose time.

He faces the audience.

George Leigh Mallory. Perhaps you've heard of me. I've been getting mentioned too often in the papers for my liking. *The Times* kept a close eye on the '21 and '22 expeditions and they're watching this one hard as well. Everyone's convinced the 1924 expedition's the one that's finally going to crack it; get to the top. And we will. I'm going to be the first man ever to climb Everest. The first ever to climb Chomolungma – Goddess Mother of the World.

The white light fades in and out as we hear Sharon, Jim's mum from off stage.

Sharon Jim, I can't look after you, I can't.

Jim falters at the front of the stage.

Jim I'll climb it. I will climb it.

Sharon I'm sorry Jim. You'll be better off without me.

There is a last blast of wind as Jim runs to the side of the stage. The drapes are flown out to reveal, on one side, the Welland's kitchen and on the other, a back gate and the back entrance of a fast food takeaway shop with a couple of dustbins outside and a neutral space downstage. Only the front of the stage is lit as Tony, Jim's social worker crosses towards Jim, who is outside a children's home.

Tony Jim! I've been looking all over for you.

Jim What?

Tony Daydreaming again? Let me guess. About Everest, right?

Jim What do you want?

Tony You should be getting yourself ready. I'm picking you up this afternoon to take you to your new foster-parents, remember? Mr and Mrs Welland.

Jim groans.

Jim Oh no.

Tony They're looking forward to you coming to live with them. And you'll be seeing their daughter Miranda for the first time.

Jim I don't want to. I want to go and live back with my mum.

Tony Let's not go over all that again Jim. You know your mum's not able to look after you any more.

Jim Why not? There's nothing wrong with her, is there?

Tony Just make sure you're ready for two o'clock when I pick you up. You have got your bags packed, haven't you?

Jim No.

Tony Well go in and pack them.

Jim I can't. Not now. I'm going out.

Tony Where?

Jim Just out.

Jim goes off. Tony calls after him.

Tony Make sure you're ready for two o'clock.

Scene Two

The lights come up on the Welland's kitchen and Miranda enters, carrying a shopping bag which she dumps on the table.

She starts emptying the shopping onto the table, but stops when she brings out a cereal packet with a 'free gift inside' offer emblazoned over it. She reads.

Miranda 'Glow in the Dark Eyes'. Big deal. That's for kids.

She continues emptying the shopping, but is drawn back to the packet. She tries to open it discreetly and looks unsuccessfully in it for the free gift. She gets a cereal bowl and pours some out. She still can't find the gift. Inspired, she gets a large bowl from the shelves and pours out the whole packet. She picks out the 'horror eyes' and puts them on.

I'm Tharg from the planet Warg.

She bangs into the table and removes the eyes.

What a load of rubbish.

We hear Mr and Mrs Welland approaching.

Mr Welland All I'm saying is, it's going to be a bit of an upheaval.

Mrs Welland Alan, we've been through all of this.

Miranda dashes to the large bowl and tries to pour the cereal back in the box, stopping as her parents enter. They put the shopping away during the following. Mrs Welland notices the large bowl of cereal.

I didn't realise you were that hungry, Miri.

Mr Welland You're sure you're still happy about having a foster-brother, Miranda?

Miranda Yeah, I suppose.

Mr Welland You suppose? It's because you've always been going on about wanting a brother.

Miranda looks embarrassed.

Miranda Dad.

Mr Welland 'I want a brother. Why can't I have a baby brother?'

Mrs Welland Alan, it's a bit late to start worrying now.

Mr Welland I'm worried. Jim McLindon's going to be a handful.

Miranda What's wrong with him?

Mrs Welland	Nothing. Your father's just fussing as usual.
Mr Welland	He's made his mum's life hell, hasn't he?
Mrs Welland	Only since his grandmother died. She was the one who really looked after him.
Mr Welland	His last school said he was fighting all the time and when he's not fighting, he wanders round in some stupid daydream. What was it? Canoeing.
Miranda	Mountaineering.
Mrs Welland	His social worker said his great grandad had something to do with climbing Everest or something, didn't he?

Miranda points to the shopping bag.

Miranda	I got a book out of the library on it.
Mr Welland	So we're going to have two of you nuts about it now? Great.

He looks at the cereal.

Miranda, what have you been doing?

Miranda	Packet was torn.
Mrs Welland	Can both of you please get out of the kitchen and let me get lunch ready? We don't want the poor lad thinking he's come into a madhouse.
Mr Welland	That's if he doesn't turn it into one.
Mrs Welland	I'm sure Jim isn't going to be that hard to handle, dear.

Scene Three

Lights up on the back alley. Matt, the fast food takeaway owner, is standing outside his shop holding Jim by the collar. Jim is struggling like mad.

Jim	Get off! Get off, will you!

He tries to kick Matt.

Matt Watch it or I'll get Samson out here. Do you remember my dog Samson?

Jim This alley's public property.

Matt But the back of my takeway isn't, especially when you've been spitting on the windows.

Jim That wasn't me.

Matt I don't want you hanging round. That's all. All right?

He releases Jim.

Jim I'm only waiting for my mum to come home.

He points to the back gate.

That's our house.

Matt I know where she lives and I know for a fact she doesn't want you hanging round here either. Best thing your mum ever did, getting rid of you, you little toerag.

Stubby, Jim's friend who has a prosthetic boot, comes on and watches without being noticed.

Jim She didn't get rid of me. She was just a bit upset if you must know. But I'm coming back now.

Matt Dream on kid. Your mum doesn't want you; no one wants you round here.

He starts to go back into the shop.

If I can still see you out here in two minutes, I'm going to set Samson onto you. Understand?

Matt goes back into the shop. Jim lifts one of the bins and is about to tip it out when Stubby comes forward.

Stubby Jim, don't! Samson'll have your leg off.

Jim Hiya Stubbs.

He lowers the bin.

How'ya doing?

Stubby Come over here, where he can't see you . . . I hate that dog. I put superglue all over a bone for it once.

Jim Nutter.

Act One, Scene Three

Stubby   Dog didn't get near it. Bone stuck to my hand and Mum had to take me to casualty.

Jim indicates Matt.

Jim   I'd like to put him in casualty. I told Mum not to buy takeaways off him but she's always hanging round there.

Stubby   What're you doing here anyway? I thought they'd put you in a home.

Jim   I didn't like it, so I've come back.

Stubby   Your mum taken you in again?

Jim   Not yet, but she's going to.

Stubby   She's a rotten mum to throw you out in the first place.

Jim grabs hold of Stubby. He is furious.

Jim   Watch it!

Stubby   Give over! Get off!

Jim   I'll do you.

Stubby   All right, get off.

Jim lets go.

Stubby   I was only saying.

Jim   Mum's all right. She was upset, that's all. 'Cos of Gran dying. And I was upset 'cos of Gran, so we didn't get on for a bit. But we'll be all right now. The minute she listens to me, we'll be all right again.

Stubby   I hope so. It was good you living here. There's no one to hang round with any more.

Jim   What about Mickey and Deano?

Stubby   Won't let me join in anything. They call me 'Spaz' and 'Plastic Man'.

He lifts his prosthetic boot in explanation.

Jim   They never used to.

Stubby   'Cos you were here to stick up for me.

Jim   You gotta learn to stick up for yourself Stubbs.

Stubby I know. But I wouldn't mind it if you still lived round here.

Jim's mum comes down the alley. She pretends not to see Jim and hurries off through her back gate. Jim sees her and chases after her.

Jim Mum! Mum! It's me. Don't shut the gate.

He bangs hard on the gate.

Jim Mum! I want to talk to you.

Jim comes away from the gate and goes to the bins. He picks up two bin-lids and speaks to Stubby.

She couldn't hear me.

Jim takes the bin-lids to the back gate and starts banging them together.

Mum! It's me, Jim!

Stubby Give up, will you.

Jim Come on, Mum!

He bangs the lids again. Matt comes on.

Matt You don't take telling, do you?

He calls.

Samson!

There is a ferocious growl. Jim runs downstage. Matt and Stubby go off.

Scene Four

We hear the sound of a light wind. Jim is picked out in a white spotlight. He stops running and pants for a few moments. When he looks up, he is happy but preoccupied. He speaks from the front of the stage.

Jim It's not as easy as you think. We've hired fifty-five Tibetan porters to get our gear to the foot of Chomolungma. We've got heaps of stuff. Tents, sleeping-bags, ice-axes and these bottles of oxygen.

It's not like taking a stroll up your nearest hill. Getting to the top is a regular job of work. The real journey starts from here. Camp Three. We've got three more camps to make higher up the mountain before we set out for the top. Each camp has to be properly prepared. Tents set up. Food put in place. Don't mention food. Horrible stuff. Tins of sardines. Macaroni. Pemmican. Pemmican's dried meat and fat stuck together. Horrible. But if it keeps you going, you'll eat anything. I'm not going to stop till I'm up there. On top of Chomolungma.

Scene Five

Tony speaks from off stage.

Tony Come on Jim.

We lose the spotlight and the wind as Tony enters with Jim's bag.

Where've you been? I've had to pack everything for you. We're due at the Wellands.

Jim looks in his bag.

Jim Where's my poster?

Tony Come on, we're running late.

Jim Where've you put it?

Tony They're expecting us at two.

Jim I'm not going without the poster.

Tony looks resigned to waiting.

Tony It's still up on the wall.

Jim goes off to collect it.

I'd been hoping you'd forget about it.

Scene Six

Tony follows Jim off as the lights come up on the Wellands. Mrs Welland is mixing a salad, while Miranda is engrossed in her book at the table.

Mrs Welland Is it good?

Miranda grunts.

Mrs Welland Does it mention, who is it? Mallory. The one Jim's meant to be interested in.

Miranda grunts again.

At least you'll have something to talk about.

Mr Welland enters, slightly flustered.

Mr Welland They're here. Tony's parking outside.

He starts trying to tidy the table.

Mrs Welland Relax will you, Alan?

The doorbell sounds. Mr Welland goes off to answer it. Miranda hides the book. Mrs Welland crosses her fingers.

Here goes.

Jim enters, clutching a rolled-up poster. Tony and Mr Welland follow. Jim is trying to look his most yobbish and succeeds in unnerving the Wellands somewhat. He takes a disapproving look round the room. Mrs Welland goes over to him.

Hello Jim.

Jim ignores her. Tony looks disapproving.

Tony Jim.

Jim responds in a lifeless way.

Jim Hello.

Mr Welland goes to take the poster.

Mr Welland Shall I take that?

Jim defends the poster.

Mrs Welland You're just in time for lunch. You too, Tony.

Act One, Scene Six

Jim I don't like it here.
Tony Give it a chance will you?
He turns to Mrs Welland.
Thanks.
Tony sits down. Jim follows suit as do Miranda and Mr Welland. Jim puts his poster by the table.
Mr Welland Introduce yourself, Miranda.
Miranda Hello Jim.
Jim grunts something.
Tony I think this is going to take everyone a bit of time.
Mrs Welland Of course.
Mrs Welland puts a large bowl of food in the middle of the table.
I bet you're starving Jim.
Jim looks suspiciously at the bowl.
Jim No.
Mrs Welland Well, I hope you don't mind us eating.
She starts serving up.
Mr Welland It's couscous. Sort of an African meal. It's made from ... what's it made from?
Mrs Welland Semolina. Have you had it before, Jim?
Jim No.
Mrs Welland Oh.
Jim But my hamster did.
Mrs Welland Oh?
Jim Then it died.
Mr Welland We weren't sure what you'd like to eat. We're vegetarian.
Jim looks appalled.
Jim What?
Miranda We don't eat meat.
Tony I did tell you.

Jim No beefburgers, no sausages, no bacon?

Mrs Welland Of course, you'll be able to eat whatever you want.

Jim stands up.

Jim Beam me up, Scotty.

Tony Jim, we've talked about this. You're not going to feel settled straightaway. It's just as strange for the Wellands, remember. You've got to get used to each other.

Jim I don't want to get used. I don't want to be here.

Jim walks away from the table and looks out of the window.

Mr Welland We've managed to get you into Miranda's school. It's a very good one.

Jim I liked my old school.

Tony You were hardly ever there.

Jim I don't want another school.

Mrs Welland You might find you like it. Miranda does.

Miranda It's all right.

Jim Your garden's crap.

Mr Welland Nobody's perfect, Jim.

Jim turns to Tony.

Jim Can I go back to the home?

Tony You've made your mind up you're not going to like it here, haven't you?

Jim It's not me. It's this place. It's horrible.

Tony It's not your mum's home I know. But if you give it a chance, you'll start to enjoy yourself.

Jim No I won't. I won't ever enjoy it here. I hate it already.

Tony gets up and goes over to Jim.

Tony Shall we see how it goes for a week? Are you prepared to try and get along with the Wellands for a few days?

Mrs Welland We really are glad to have you here, Jim.

Act One, Scene Six

Jim shrugs his shoulders.

Tony It'll give you a chance to find your feet.

Jim When am I going to see Mum again?

Tony I'll try and fix something up.

Jim I want to see her. You're my social worker. You're meant to sort that out. I want to see her.

Tony I'll do what I can. She's got to want to see you as well, you know.

Jim Sort it out.

Tony moves away from Jim.

Tony I've got to make a move. That was delicious, Mrs Welland. Are you sure you'll be . . .

Mrs Welland We'll be fine.

Mr Welland We'll see you out.

Tony Give it a chance, eh Jim?

Jim ignores him. Tony, Mr and Mrs Welland go out. Jim stands looking out of the window. Miranda watches him.

Miranda There's a football team at school, if you're any good at football.

No response from Jim.

Most of the teachers are mad, but the kids are all right. They're a good laugh, some of them. What was your old school like?

Still no response.

I bet you're missing your mum. I don't blame you. I'd miss mine.

Still no response. Miranda gets up and takes the horror eyes out of a pocket.

I wish you wouldn't talk so much. You're making the eyes pop out of my head.

She puts the eyes on and walks towards Jim. She mimics him.

I hate it already. I'm not going to like it. I'm never going to like it.

Jim responds angrily.

Jim Are you taking the mickey?

Jim turns round and is taken aback by Miranda's appearance. He half laughs in spite of himself. Miranda answers defiantly.

Miranda Yes, I am.

She takes off the horror eyes and goes back to the table.

What's your poster of?

Jim goes over to it.

Jim Leave it alone.

Miranda All right. I only wanted to look. What is it?

Jim Chomolungma.

Miranda What?

Jim unrolls it.

Jim Mount Everest, stupid. It's really called Chomolungma.

Miranda It'd look nice on the cupboard. There's some sticky stuff still on the back.

She goes to put up the poster.

Jim I'll do it.

Jim puts the poster up.

Miranda It's nice.

Jim Mum bought it me.

Miranda What's she like, your mum? I bet she's nice.

Jim She's all right.

Miranda Why doesn't she want you?

Jim I dunno.

Miranda It's not very nice of her.

Jim is angry.

Jim She's all right.

Miranda	She might take you back one day.
Jim	She will do. Soon as I talk to her, she'll take me back and I'll be out of this place. Away from you and your lousy parents.
Miranda	Charming.
Jim	I don't want to be here.
Miranda	How do you think I feel? I've got to put up with you here and at school.
Jim	I'm not going near you at school.
Miranda	We're in the same class.

Scene Seven

Mrs Pryme, a teacher at St Xavier's, comes on. We are in the playground of the Comprehensive. She looks at her watch and takes out a whistle, ready to blow. Before she can do so, another teacher, Mr Cooper hurries on.

Mr Cooper	Hang on, Janice. Give me a minute to get to class and get some notes up on the board.
Mrs Pryme	As well prepared as ever, Harry?
Mr Cooper	Don't you start. I've just had the Head bending my ear because I can't stay for the staff meeting this evening.
Mrs Pryme	You're not trying to wriggle out of it, are you?
Mr Cooper	I've got to get my car back from the garage and it closes at five.
Mrs Pryme	I bet Mr Bryant loved that.

Mr Cooper mimics the Head.

Mr Cooper	'You have to try and organise your life appropriately, Mr Cooper. The rest of the staff manage to organise things so they can attend staff meetings.'
Mrs Pryme	A bit of a pain?
Mr Cooper	'A bit of a pain' is putting it mildly.

Mr Bryant, the Headmaster, comes on behind Mr Cooper. Mrs Pryme tries to signal this unsuccessfully.

He's the most pompous, over-opinionated, windbag of a . . . ow!

Mrs Pryme has kicked him, as Mr Bryant draws level.

Head We're running a little late, aren't we, Mrs Pryme? I make it one minute past nine.

Mrs Pryme I'm getting them in now.

Mrs Pryme blows the whistle as Mr Cooper slinks off.

Come on now, quickly, go straight in, straight in. Come on now.

Mrs Pryme goes off. The Head waits for a moment at the edge of the playground. Miranda hurries on at the opposite side.

Miranda Hurry up, Jim. Hurry up!

Jim comes on in no particular rush.

Head You're late, Miranda.

Miranda Yes, Sir, sorry Sir.

Head Why's that?

Miranda I was showing Jim the way to school.

Head So you're Jim McLindon?

Jim Yes.

Head Yes, Sir.

Jim Sir.

Head Go in, Miranda.

Miranda goes off.

I was just looking through the reports on you from your last school, Jim. They don't make very impressive reading, do they?

Jim Don't they, Sir?

Head No, they don't. Not by a long chalk. You have a reputation for being a truant; or turning up late when you could be bothered to come.

Jim That was only after my gran . . .

Act One, Scene Seven

Head I didn't ask you to say anything. If I want you to speak, I'll let you know. Now let's get something straight on your first day here, McLindon. This school sets itself very high standards. We're top of just about every performance table in the district and we want to keep it that way. So we expect very high standards from our pupils as well and come down hard on those who don't like to conform. Do I make myself clear?

Jim mumbles.

Jim Sir.

Head Pardon?

Jim Yes, Sir.

Head I hope so, McLindon. For your sake. Now where are you supposed to be?

Jim I don't know, Sir.

Head Go through to the office.

He indicates off stage.

They'll tell you. And I hope I don't have to speak to you again.

The Head goes off. Jim is left alone onstage. The lights start to go to white and a wind begins, stopping abruptly as Miranda comes back on.

Miranda Come on. We've got Personal Development.

Jim What?

Miranda Personal Development with Mrs Pryme. She kills you if you're late.

Jim and Miranda go off as Mrs Pryme comes on followed by Peter, a pupil, carrying chairs, which he puts out. Miranda and Jim hurry on.

Mrs Pryme Good morning, Three G . . . You must be James McLindon?

Jim Jim.

Mrs Pryme Jim. It's nice to have you in the class, Jim.

Jim doesn't react. Mrs Pryme addresses the whole class.

Now, I hope you've all had a think about your personal ambitions over the weekend, as I asked you to. Peter, what about you? Have you thought about your future?

Peter Yes, Miss.

Mrs Pryme What are your hopes?

Peter Well, Miss, I intend staying on in the sixth form to take Economics, Geography and English 'A' Level. I'm going to work very hard at them, so I expect to go on to university; hopefully Oxford or Cambridge, though I mustn't be too choosy. At University, I'll study Politics, Philosophy and Economics.

Mrs Pryme Very good.

Peter continues hurriedly.

Peter And while I'm there, I hope to meet a nice girl to marry, because I'm going to need a good wife who'll help me in my chosen career as a politician.

Jim puts his fingers down his throat.

Mrs Pryme Is there something the matter, Jim?

Jim No, Miss.

Peter continues as though nothing can stop him.

Peter And I hope to become a member of the Cabinet and have a Persian cat, a labrador and three children or some goldfish.

Mrs Pryme That was very good, Peter. What about you, Miranda?

Miranda I'm not sure what I want to do, Miss, but I think I want to work with children.

Mrs Pryme Would you like to be a teacher?

Miranda Perhaps. Or a social worker. I'd like to help children with problems no one else can help.

Jim mimes being violently ill.

Mrs Pryme That's a very interesting idea to have, Miranda, but it

Act One, Scene Seven

Jim   doesn't seem to meet with Jim's approval. Tell us, what are your plans for the future, Jim?

Jim   I haven't got any.

Mrs Pryme   Don't you ever think about what you're going to be in a few years' time?

Jim   A layabout.

Peter sniggers.

Mrs Pryme   That's not much of an ambition, is it? I think that's what some people have told you you'll be and you've believed them. Isn't there someone in your family who does something you'd like to do? Your dad, or an uncle or someone?

Jim   I don't know who my dad was. I expect he was a layabout as well.

Peter   You don't know who your dad was!

Mrs Pryme   And there's no one you admire? No one you'd like to be like?

Jim   No.

Miranda   Miss, one of Jim's relatives climbed up Everest.

Jim   No, he didn't.

Miranda   That's what Tony said.

Jim   My great grandad was a steward on the boat that took George Mallory to India on his way to Everest, if you must know.

Mrs Pryme   Really?

Jim   Yeah. He used to serve Mallory his meals and all that.

Mrs Pryme   That's fascinating. Does anyone know who George Mallory was. Peter?

Peter   No, Miss.

Mrs Pryme   He was a very famous mountaineer. Some people say he was the first man to climb Everest, but he disappeared before he came down, so no one knows if he really got to the top or not. Are there any souvenirs in the family of all this? Any photos?

Jim   There's a couple of letters he sent my great grandma.

Peter	Liar.
Jim	Shut up!
Mrs Pryme	Peter, don't be so rude.
Peter	I bet he's just making it up to impress you, Miss.
Jim	Shut your face.
Mrs Pryme	Jim, don't take any notice. What did your great grandfather say in his letter?
Jim	Nothing much. He couldn't write very well. He just said he was sure Mallory'd make it to the top. He could stand all the cold and climbing 'cos he was hard as rock himself.
Mrs Pryme	So would you like to work as a steward one day, Jim?
Jim	No. I want to climb Everest.
Peter	Miss, when I'm Prime Minister, I'm going to make it illegal to tell lies.

Jim gives Peter a filthy look. The lesson bell goes. Mrs Pryme and the children go off.

Scene Eight

Sharon McLindon's home. Her hairdressing equipment is out, ready to be packed into carrying cases. Sharon enters, followed by Tony. Sharon carries on preparing to go out.

Tony	Thanks for agreeing to see me, Mrs McLindon.
Sharon	It's all right.
Tony	I can see you're busy.
Sharon	I'm giving an old lady a rinse and perm in fifteen minutes.
Tony	If you'd rather I came back another time . . .
Sharon	You've got something to say, haven't you? So say it.
Tony	Jim's keen to see you, Mrs McLindon.

Act One, Scene Eight

Sharon just carries on.

He really does want to see you.

Sharon I'd love to see him, but it's too early, in't it? He hasn't had time to settle in with the . . . who did you say they were?

Tony The Wellands.

Sharon He's got to get used to them. If he saw me now, he'd think there was a chance of coming back.

Tony I think it's important you stay in touch with him.

Sharon stops packing.

Sharon I know it's important! Don't talk to me like I'm thick or something . . .

Tony I'm sorry if . . .

Sharon Jim's my son. I know. My responsibility. But I had him too young. I was sixteen. What sort of life do you think I've had since then? Have you thought about that?

Tony No one's trying to accuse you of anything, Mrs McLindon.

Sharon Well it feels like you are. But you're not going to make me feel guilty. Because I don't. I'm doing the right thing. I'm making a life for myself at last.

Tony Perhaps you could phone him. He'd appreciate a phone call.

Sharon It'd upset him.

Tony I don't think so . . .

Sharon Then it'd upset me. I've had to cope with my mother dying. It's not easy setting up this business and there's . . . other things in my life.

Tony I know. I understand . . . All the same, how would it be if I picked you up on Saturday morning? Took you round to the Wellands for an hour, just to talk?

Sharon You don't give up, do you?

Tony Will you at least think about it? For Jim's sake?

Sharon	I've got to go out.
Tony	I'll give you a ring later in the week.

Scene Nine

Lights up on Mr Cooper who is dressed in an outrageous shellsuit and carrying a cassette recorder, which he switches on. He starts performing some eurythmics to new age music. He looks ridiculous.

Peter, one of the pupils, dressed expensively, comes on and joins in enthusiastically. Miranda, also well presented, comes on and is about to join in, when Jim enters. He is dressed in a heavy metal T-shirt and cut-off jeans. He looks in amazement.

Jim	Bloody 'ell.
	He goes up to Miranda.
	What's all this?
Miranda	Eurythmics. Movement to music.
Jim	Dancing like the fairies, more like.
Mr Cooper	No talking. Come round here and join in.
	Mr Cooper looks at Jim's clothes distastefully. He switches off the music and tugs at the T-shirt.
	What do you call this, James?
Jim	We call it a T-shirt on my planet, Sir.
Mr Cooper	Don't try and be insolent . . . Well, boys and girls, it seems we've had a trendsetter join the school. All these years I've asked pupils to turn up in clean smart sports clothes, it seems I've been mistaken. You should've been coming in dirty old jeans with the legs cut off.
	Peter sniggers dutifully.
Jim	No one said anything at my last school.
Mr Cooper	No, I don't imagine they did. But you're at St Xavier's

	now and we do things differently here. I'm sure your mother would be horrified to know that you were the scruffiest boy in the class, wouldn't she?
Miranda	Sir . . .
Mr Cooper	Be quiet, Miranda. I take it your mother does take an interest in the way you look, doesn't she, Jim? I'm sure she cares about you.
	Jim kicks the cassette recorder over and runs off.
	Come back here. Come back at once, McLindon!
Miranda	That's not fair, Sir. Jim's staying with us at the moment and my mum couldn't buy him anything till she knew his size.
Mr Cooper	Were you asked to speak, Miranda Welland?
Miranda	No, Sir.
Mr Cooper	Then don't. I'll let the Head know about Master McLindon's behaviour later. In the meantime, let's all relax and flow in harmony to the music.

Scene Ten

Lights come up on the Welland's kitchen.

Mr Welland is working on some papers at the table. Mrs Welland comes in with a large sports shop carrier bag.

Mrs Welland	Darling, what do you think of these?
	She takes a selection of sports clothes out of the bag.
Mr Welland	Very nice.
Mrs Welland	I hope Jim likes them. And I've bought a mountain of beefburgers.
Mr Welland	Anything to cheer him up. He had a face like a dead dolphin going off to school this morning.
Mrs Welland	Poor lad.
Mr Welland	Miserable little so and so.

Mrs Welland looks disapproving.

Mrs Welland Alan.

Mr Welland He could make some effort, couldn't he?

Miranda enters with school bag.

Mrs Welland Miri, look at these. They're for Jim.

She holds up the sports clothes.

Miranda Not bad. It's a pity he didn't have them today. Mr Cooper really showed him up for not having the right stuff and then the Head gave him a telling off after school.

Mrs Welland That's not fair.

Miranda The Head's never fair.

Mr Welland Where's Jim now?

Miranda He went straight upstairs. He's in a bit of a mood. It was a real telling off.

Mrs Welland goes to the door.

Mrs Welland Jim, can you come down a moment?

She comes back into the kitchen and picks up the sports clothes.

He'll look as smart as Linford Christie.

Miranda Linford Lunchbox.

Mr Welland Miri.

Jim comes in.

Mrs Welland Look at these, love. What do you think?

Jim shrugs.

Mr Welland These cost a bit, you know.

Mrs Welland I'm sorry you didn't have them for today. Miranda said you got into a bit of bother about it.

Jim Nothing I couldn't handle.

Mr Welland I hope you didn't use that tone with the Headmaster.

Mrs Welland Do you want to go and try them on?

Jim Not especially.

Act One, Scene Ten

Mrs Welland I'll need to get them changed if they don't fit. It'd only take you a minute.

Jim I don't want to.

Mr Welland Jim, do as you're told!

With a great sigh, Jim takes the clothes and goes upstairs.

Mrs Welland There was no need to lose your temper with him.

Mr Welland He seems to think everyone exists to run after him. Did I tell you his social worker was on the phone earlier?

Mrs Welland No.

Mr Welland He's finally persuaded Jim's mum to come round and see him.

Mrs Welland That's good.

Miranda I wonder what she's like.

Mr Welland We'll find out on Saturday. It's probably best if I take you ice-skating then to give them a bit of privacy.

Miranda Oh! I wanted to see what she looks like.

Mrs Welland speaks to Miranda.

Mrs Welland Jim's all right, isn't he?

Miranda He's OK.

Mr Welland As long as you don't start picking up his bad habits.

Miranda What would you be like, Dad, if you were in a strange house and at a strange school?

Mrs Welland Exactly. He's just frightened.

Mr Welland I hope so. Because I'm beginning to wonder if it was such a good idea having him come here after all.

Mrs Welland It'll just take time.

Jim comes in with the clothes in the bag.

Mrs Welland Well?

Jim They didn't fit.

Mrs Welland Never mind. We can get them changed.

Jim So I tried to make them fit. With the scissors.

He takes the clothes out. He's deliberately shredded them and they hang in tatters.

Mr Welland How dare you!
Mrs Welland Alan . . .
Miranda What did you do that for?
Mr Welland Have you any idea how much they cost?
Mrs Welland Alan!

She speaks deliberately.

We can always buy you some more clothes, Jim.
Jim Then you're going to need to buy a lot. I'm good with scissors.

Scene Eleven

Tony and Sharon enter. They're on the street outside the Wellands'. Sharon is admiring the outside of the house.

Sharon It's beautiful.
Tony Quite nice.
Sharon No, it's beautiful. It's a really beautiful house.
Tony We ought to go in. We're rather late as it is.
Sharon He's never lived anywhere like this. Look, I shouldn't've come. I'll only show him up.
Tony No, you won't, Mrs McLindon. He'll be really pleased to see you.
Sharon I shouldn't've listened to you.
Tony He's expecting you now. Let's go in.
Sharon I want you there all the time. Don't leave me alone with him.

Scene Twelve

Lights up on the Wellands' kitchen. Jim's brushing his hair. He's very nervous. The doorbell goes. Jim puts the brush away. He tries to find a position to stay in. Mrs Welland comes into the room.

Mrs Welland Visitors.

She shows Sharon and Tony in, then withdraws.

Jim You're late.

Tony Unavoidable.

There is a slight pause.

Sharon Hello, Jim.

Jim moves towards his mum. She ignores this and sits down at the table. Tony finds a corner.

How've you been?

Jim All right.

Sharon What's your new school like?

Jim All right, I suppose.

Sharon looks round the kitchen.

Sharon Nice here.

Jim It's OK.

Sharon It's more than OK. It's nice. Real nice.

Jim Mum.

Sharon You'll love it here, I bet.

Jim Mum.

Sharon It's much better than my tatty old dump, isn't it?

Jim Can I come home?

Sharon sighs.

Sharon No, Jim.

Jim Go on, Mum. I'll be good.

Sharon No.

Jim Why not?

Sharon	We'd drive each other mad.
Jim	We wouldn't.
Sharon	You drove me mad after Gran died. I couldn't handle it.
Jim	It'd be different.

Sharon speaks to Tony.

Sharon	He was fighting; shoplifting, everything.
Jim	I was upset.
Sharon	You think I wasn't?
Jim	You're my mum. I want to live with you.

Sharon speaks to Tony again.

Sharon	I thought he understood he can't come back.
Tony	That's not what this morning's about, Jim.

Jim speaks to Sharon.

Jim	I hate it here.
Sharon	Can't you find him anywhere else?
Jim	I'd hate it anywhere. I want to go home.
Tony	Your mother feels she wouldn't be able to look after you properly, Jim.
Jim	I'd look after myself.
Sharon	I'm working all hours now. The hairdressing's really taken off.

Jim speaks to Tony.

Jim	You tell her. Mums are meant to look after their children, aren't they? That's what mums are for.

Sharon gets up. We hear a door open offstage. She speaks to Tony.

Sharon	Why don't you get in touch with his father, if you can find him? He hasn't done anything for Jim in twelve years.

Miranda comes bursting into the kitchen carrying a pair of iceskates.

Miranda	Whoo! I'm starving!

We hear Mrs Welland speak from off stage.

Mrs Welland Miri!

Miranda sees what's happening.

Miranda Soz. Don't mind me.

Sharon gets ready to leave.

Jim Don't go yet, Mum.

Sharon speaks to Tony.

Sharon I knew it'd be a waste of time coming round.

She fishes in her purse and takes out a tenner.

Look, Jim, this is for you. Buy yourself something nice.

Jim I want to go home, Mum. I want to go home.

Sharon stands uncertainly for a moment, then shakes her head.

Sharon I'm sorry . . . I'm sorry.

She puts the money on the table and hurries out, brushing past Miranda.

Jim Mum!

Jim stands in shock. Tony moves towards him.

Tony Jim, I know you must feel awful.

Jim Shut up! This is all your lousy fault!

He dashes off.

Scene Thirteen

The Himalayan winds start gusting very strongly as the neutral area is bathed in white light. Jim comes into the light and addresses the audience from the front of the stage.

Jim I never expected it to be easy. Climbing any mountain's hard, but this one, Chomolungma, is the hardest thing in the world. So I'm caught in a little tent at twenty-six thousand feet; the wind's trying to blow me clean off the mountain and the snow is gusting over in sheets. So what? I have to sit tight for another day, that's all.

He tugs at his collar and continues.

It's getting hard to breathe ... The oxygen's thin here and it's going to get worse. When the blizzard ends and I start out again, every step's going to be a nightmare – the mountain's treacherous. You see what looks like a nice easy route and set off, crunching across the snow like a Boxing Day Walk. But there's ice under the snow and you can slip. An avalanche'll start and you're swept away, hundreds of feet in a matter of seconds.

Between here and the top, death is sitting and watching – deciding whether to let me pass by, or catch hold of me for daring the impossible. To climb Chomolungma, you have to risk everything. Everything.

The wind gusts. Then we lose the white light as Jim goes off.

Scene Fourteen

The lights come up on the dustbins and the alley. Stubby is playing with a basketball and gives the following commentary.

Stubby And it's Jordan again. It's like the ball's tied to his hand. He's dribbling round everyone and that's with his eyes closed ... But surely even Jordan can't score from here.

Stubby lifts a bin-lid and slam-dunks the ball in. He celebrates.

That's an incredible fifty points to Michael Jordan and they've only been playing for five minutes.

Act One, Scene Fourteen

Jim comes on as Stubby takes the ball out of the bin.

Jim Stubbs!

Stubby passes the ball to Jim. They interchange a couple of passes, then Jim throws the ball close to the Takeaway window and Stubby has to make a desperate save.

Stubby Careful!

Jim Do him good to have his window out.

Stubby, very deliberately, sits down with the ball. Jim comes and sits next to him.

Stubby What're you doing here?

Jim Nothing.

Stubby Come to see your mum?

Jim Seen her.

Stubby She taking you back?

Jim shrugs.

I bet she'll be round here soon. She's always hanging round there these days.

He indicates the Takeway.

Jim I just wanted to get out. They drive me mad where I am.

Stubby My mum's doing my head in an' all. 'Get your room tidied up. It looks like the Corporation Tip'.

Jim They make me sick. I ripped up all these clothes they bought me and they didn't even get mad.

Stubby What you do that for?

Jim And there's a girl. Miranda. She's horrible.

Stubby Yeah. Girls usually are.

Jim It's really boring there.

Stubby It's really boring here.

Jim Well, let's do something.

Stubby What?

Jim	I dunno.
Stubby	You're the one with ideas.
	Jim thinks for a moment, then grabs the basketball. He holds it up like a globe and points.
Jim	There.
Stubby	What?
Jim	Tibet. The Himalayas.
Stubby	You what?
Jim	We're going to the Himalayas to climb Mount Everest.
Stubby	I promised me mam I'd be back for tea.
Jim	It's a game, you daft chissick. We could do it in the Quarry. I'll be George Mallory and you can be his best mate, Sandy Irvine.
Stubby	OK.
Jim	They both disappeared on the mountain.
Stubby	I don't want to disappear. We've got a 'Star Trek' video for tonight.
Jim	All right. You can be Odell. He got back off the mountain . . . We can pretend that big, sticky-out bit of rock is Everest . . . I've never seen anyone climb out on that. We can be the first.
Stubby	What about my leg?
Jim	What about it? If you could get up there, all the other kids'd have to shut up calling you 'Plastic Man'.
Stubby	All right, let's go.
	Miranda enters.
Miranda	Where're you off to?
Jim	What you doing here?
Miranda	I'm just here.
Jim	Well go away again.
Stubby	Who is she?
Miranda	Where're you going?
Jim	Somewhere that doesn't concern little girls.

Act One, Scene Fourteen

Miranda Oh, I am sorry. I didn't recognise you, Mr Schwarzenegger.

Stubby Come on.

Jim wants to make a point in front of Miranda. He speaks to Stubby.

Jim Yeah. As soon as I've scored one past you. In there.

Jim points to the bin. He starts showing off with the basketball, then tries dribbling round Stubby. They have a tussle which leads to Stubby crashing into the bins. Matt comes out, enraged.

Matt What the bloody hell are you playing at?

Jim It was an accident.

Matt You're not wanted round here. Now clear off and take your little spastic friend with you.

Jim is furious.

Jim Don't call him that!

Matt Well he is, isn't he?

Jim Don't ever call him that.

Stubby Let's get off.

Matt Now move it.

Jim I'll get you for that. For calling him that.

Matt Oh yeah?

He calls.

Samson, Samson!

A rottweiller growls offstage. Stubby grabs Jim's arm and pulls him offstage. Matt looks at Miranda.

You don't want to hang round with him. He belongs in here . . .

He indicates the bin.

With the rest of the rubbish.

Miranda goes off in the direction Jim and Stubby took. Matt goes off.

Scene Fifteen

The Quarry – a large structure with different levels is brought on. There are odd bits of junk by the foot of it – part of a bicycle, some tin cans, a length of rope. Jim enters, followed by Stubby.

Jim Base camp.

Stubby What?

Jim We'll stop here for a bit.

Stubby Oh good. I'm knackered.

Stubby sinks down on the ground by the rubbish and looks through it rather absently.

Jim We can't stop too long. The weather conditions'll be against an attempt on the summit.

Stubby You what?

Jim It's going to pee down in a minute. We'll have to set up some camps on the mountain. We can't get to the top all in one go. We've got to put up tents and lay in supplies part way up.

Stubby We haven't got any tents.

Jim Use your imagination. This is Mount Everest – a huge ferocious mountain.

Stubby It's Bailey's Quarry, where everyone dumps everyone else's bike.

Stubby picks up the rope and twirls it round his head.

Yee-ha!

Jim Stubbs! You're a genius.

Stubby No, I'm a Capricorn. My birthday's January the eighth.

Jim grabs the rope. Miranda enters unnoticed.

Jim This'll be perfect. Come on.

Stubby I'll carry on playing when I've had a rest. I'm starving. You got anything to eat?

Jim No.

Act One, Scene Fifteen

Miranda holds out some bars of chocolate.

Miranda Have one of these.

Stubby takes a piece.

Stubby Ta.

Miranda offers one to Jim.

Miranda Want one? You can pretend it's pemmican.

Jim What're you doing here?

Miranda Thought I'd take a walk.

Jim You been following us?

Miranda offers the chocolate to Jim again.

Miranda Do you want one or not?

Jim takes it.

Jim What do you mean, I can pretend it's pemmican?

Stubby Don't introduce me, or owt polite like that.

Miranda I'm Miranda Welland.

Stubby I'm Terry Redshaw. Everyone calls me Stubby.

He speaks to Jim.

She's not horrible.

Miranda What?

Stubby Not that Jim said you were.

Jim How do you know about pemmican?

Miranda You're climbing Everest, aren't you? That's one of the things they ate.

Jim Yeah, but how do you know?

Miranda I read about it in a book. About George Mallory.

Jim You've read about him?

Miranda Yeah.

Jim He was brilliant. Did you know that my great grandad . . .

Miranda Was on the boat that took Mallory to India? Yeah, I think you've told everyone in town that.

Jim I never met anyone who's read about Mallory before.

Stubby	So they all ate chocolate and called it pemmican. Why?
Miranda	Pemmican's dried meat and fat.
Jim	It lasts for ever. That's why they take it on expeditions.
Stubby	It's very nice. Have you got any more of them pemmican bars?
Jim	Come on! If we don't hurry, a blizzard'll set in.
Stubby	Wish I'd put me vest on.
Miranda	Can I join in?
Jim	There weren't any girls on the Everest expedition.
Miranda	There weren't any thirteen-year-old boys either.
Stubby	He's Mallory, I'm Odell. Who are you going to be?
Miranda	I'll be Sandy Irvine. I'll be in charge of the oxygen masks.
Stubby	You know you have to mysteriously disappear if you're Irvine.
Jim	I wish she would.
Stubby	Let's get cracking then. Who's going up first?
Jim	Odell's got to be first. He takes supplies to the last camp before the summit so Irvine and Mallory don't have to carry so much.
Stubby	Cheers.
Jim	You wanted to be Odell. You can make a camp there.

Jim points up to a ledge on the quarry.

Stubby	What supplies am I going to take up?

Miranda holds out the last chocolate bar.

Miranda	I've got this.
Jim	Right, that'll do. And no eating it on the way up.

Miranda takes off her cardigan.

Miranda	And we can use my cardigan for a flag.

Act One, Scene Fifteen

Jim goes to the foot of the quarry, carrying the rope.

Jim Get a move on.

Stubby Listen to him.

Jim climbs to the first level, followed by Stubby then Miranda.

Jim Careful, the ice is treacherous.

Stubby looks down. He is suffering from vertigo already.

Stubby I shouldn't be up here. I get dizzy standing on a brick.

Jim Right. We're roping up.

He puts the rope round his waist, ties it on, feeds it out and then starts to tie it round Stubby.

Stubby Yow! You're tickling.

Jim Now, I want you to go up and make Camp Six.

Stubby Do I have to?

Jim We'll pass the flag up to you.

Miranda Stubby shouldn't go first.

Jim Why not?

Miranda Because of his . . .

Miranda trails off as she becomes aware of Stubby waiting for her answer.

Jim Go on, Odell. I'll give you a leg up. You've a couple of decent handholds there.

Stubby Right, Mallory.

Stubby makes his ascent to the next level. For someone without a disabled foot it wouldn't be that difficult, but it is a major challenge to Stubby. He's extremely nervous and falters once or twice. The others encourage him – 'Go on, Odell', 'Keep going, Stubby', etc. Finally Stubby makes it and is able to sit and get his breath back. Miranda and Jim cheer.

Miranda Well done!

Stubby It was a piece of cake actually.

Jim Now make the camp. Here!

He takes Miranda's cardigan and throws it up to Stubby.

Put the chocolate under a rock.

Stubby   Do I have to?

Miranda   We can share it later.

Reluctantly Stubby stashes the chocolate.

Jim   Now hold onto the rope, Odell. I'm coming up.

Stubby   Hang on, it's tea-time. Me mam'll hammer me if I'm late.

Jim   You can't just come down Everest for your tea.

Stubby   I'll have to. It's me favourite. Steaklet and chips. Give us a help down.

Stubby climbs down to the first level.

Miranda   We'd better get home as well, Jim. We'll come back another day.

Jim   All right.

He calls out.

I'll be back, Chomolungma. Back to Base camp.

They climb down to the foot of the quarry.

Stubby   That was good. I enjoyed it.

Jim   We'll get right to the top next time.

Stubby   Yeah . . . Mam'll be doing her nut. I'll see you, Jim. See you, Miranda.

Stubby hurries off. Miranda and Jim start walking, as we lose the quarry.

Miranda   I thought that would kill him, climbing up there.

Jim   Stubby?

Miranda   Yeah.

Jim   I was a bit afraid for him myself.

Miranda   Then why did you make him do it?

Jim   Dunno . . . Everyone knocks him because of his leg. It's not right. He can do all sorts when he wants to.

Act One, Scene Fifteen **39**

Miranda He did all right in the quarry . . . He's left my cardigan up there!

Jim Do you want to go back?

Miranda It's only an old one. Mum'll never notice.

Jim I bet he didn't leave the chocolate.

Miranda Why do people make fun of each other?

Jim Don't ask me.

Miranda Everyone does it though. Like Mr Cooper showing you up because of your shorts. It's not your fault your mum didn't look after you properly.

Jim Shut up!

Miranda I didn't mean it nastily. I just mean people pick on things you can't do anything about.

Jim No one makes fun of you.

Miranda You told Stubby I was horrible.

Jim Well, yeah . . .

Miranda Didn't you?

Jim I wasn't making fun. I didn't mean it. No one makes fun of you.

Miranda They would if they knew.

Jim What?

Miranda stops walking. Jim stops too.

Miranda If I tell you something, you won't ever tell anyone else?

Jim What?

Miranda You've got to promise.

Jim All right. Promise.

Miranda Sometimes my dad gets ill.

Jim So does everyone.

Miranda No. Ill up here.

She touches her head.

Jim What, mad?

Miranda No. Just, sort of depressed. He won't come out of his

	room. Mum brings him up all of his meals. She tells me he's working, like I don't know there's something wrong.
Jim	How often does it happen?
Miranda	He can go ages without it happening. Then something stupid'll set him off; he'll get upset over nothing and disappear into his room for a week.
Jim	Must be creepy for you.
Miranda	You won't ever tell anyone, will you?
Jim	No.
Miranda	Promise?
Jim	Promise.

They start walking again.

Miranda	If you ever let on at school, they'd make life hell for me.

The bins and alley are lit.

Jim	Don't worry. I keep my promises. Always.
Miranda	We'd better hurry up.
Jim	You go on home.
Miranda	What?
Jim	I'll be back soon.
Miranda	What're you going to do?
Jim	Nothing.
Miranda	Jim?
Jim	I've got to see someone, that's all. I'll be back soon. Go on.
Miranda	All right . . . We'll go up that mountain another day, yeah?
Jim	Yeah.

Reluctantly Miranda goes off. Jim goes to the alley and picks up one of the bins.

Spastic, is he? You should've seen him halfway up that quarry. You wouldn't've had the guts. I'll show you spastic.

Jim throws the bin through the Takeaway window, setting off an alarm. Jim turns and walks slowly downstage, as the lights turn to white and the alarm crossfades with the Himalayan wind. Over, we hear the following voices, repeating and overlapping.

Matt Your mum doesn't want you. No one wants you round here.

Sharon I thought he understood he wouldn't be coming back.

Mr Cooper I take it your mother does care about you, doesn't she?

Sharon Sorry . . . I'm sorry.

Jim draws into himself, becoming as small as possible as the winds gust furiously.

End of Act One.

ACT TWO

Scene One

The stage is in darkness with a high, gusting wind for some moments. A spotlight comes up on the poster of Everest. The wind fades as the lights come up on the Wellands' kitchen.

Jim is sitting on a chair downstage of the table. He is facing the audience and away from Mr and Mrs Welland, who are standing. Tony is seated at the table. Miranda is sitting cross-legged in a corner of the room, cleaning her ice-skating boots.

Jim is in disgrace. There is a long silence.

Mrs Welland That's the first time, the first time ever . . .

Mr Welland All the neighbours were at the window, couldn't see enough of it.

Mrs Welland A police car outside this house!

Mr Welland Do you know how lucky you are, Jim? . . . I said, do you know how lucky you are?

No response from Jim.

Tony Jim.

Jim shifts in his chair, half-looks back over his shoulder, then stares expressionlessly again.

Mrs Welland Smashing a window! What got into you?

Mr Welland If he'd brought charges against you, you'd have a criminal record now.

Mrs Welland I suppose you haven't thought of the money we've got to find to pay for the damage?

Tony I think you owe Mr and Mrs Welland an apology, Jim, don't you?

Jim I didn't ask them to have me.

Tony That's not the point.

Mr Welland	You're not making things any easier you know.
Miranda	It's not all his fault. That man called Jim's friend a spastic.
Mrs Welland	We're not saying the owner's not at fault.
Mr Welland	You don't try and sort things out that way. Do you think smashing his window's going to make him any better towards handicapped people?
Jim	Stubby's not handicapped!
Mr Welland	We're not talking about Stubby.
Jim	Then don't call him handicapped.

Tony addresses the Wellands.

Tony	Can I have a word with Jim in private?
Mrs Welland	Of course.

The Wellands go off. Tony goes over to Jim.

Tony	How're you feeling?
Jim	OK?
Tony	Really?
Jim	I'm OK.
Tony	You know, if your mum hadn't been able to talk the Takeaway owner out of prosecuting you, you'd be in big trouble.
Jim	So what?
Tony	It's lucky she gets on so well with him.
Jim	I wouldn't mind if the police had taken me away. I wouldn't mind if I had been put in prison. Couldn't be worse than this.
Tony	You don't know what you're talking about, Jim. The Wellands care about you, you know that?
Jim	No one asked them to.
Tony	But they do. All of them. And if you gave yourself a chance, if you stopped trying to fight the whole world, you might actually start to enjoy life a bit . . . Your mum's not going to take you back again, Jim.

	It's not going to happen. You've got to get on with the rest of your life.
Jim	I'm not bothered about my mum.
Tony	In her own way, she does still love you.
Jim	Oh yeah?
Tony	Yes . . . so why don't you give her a son that's worth loving? One who's not in trouble at school all the time. One who doesn't have the police chasing after him. You never know; if she hears you're a pretty smart lad, she might just understand what she's missing after all.

Jim looks at him for the first time.

Give it a try, eh? One time, just give it a try.

Tony puts his hand on Jim's shoulder then goes off. After a moment, Miranda comes in with her school bag, which she dumps on the table. She takes a couple of books out and starts to work.
Jim goes over to the table and looks at what she's doing. Miranda looks annoyed.

Miranda	What do you want?
Jim	Is that homework? Have we got some?
Miranda	Homework?
Jim	Yeah.
Miranda	I didn't think you bothered.
Jim	Yeah, well . . . I thought I might have a go. What is it?

Miranda is furious.

Miranda	Jim, can you just leave me alone! I've had enough of you for one day. Mum and Dad are arguing with each other again and it's all your fault.
Jim	I'm sorry, I'm sorry.
Miranda	The next thing, Dad'll get in one of his moods and do you know what happens next?
Jim	I didn't want to upset anyone.
Miranda	This house'll become hell. He'll lock himself away. He

	doesn't get dressed; he just sits in his dressing-gown for days. It's horrible.
Jim	I guess so.

Miranda is close to tears.

Miranda	Last time it happened, I went in. Mum told me not to, but I did. He was sat on the bed. He'd got some scissors in his hand and he was holding a fish or something he'd cut out of paper. All over the bed was little fish.
Jim	I didn't mean to wind everyone up.
Miranda	Well you have.
Jim	I know what it's like.
Miranda	No, you don't.
Jim	I do. My mum's really weird sometimes. Like she isn't my real mum at all. She won't talk to me. She doesn't want to know me.
Miranda	That's your problem, isn't it?
Jim	Yeah, I suppose it is. Look, what is this homework?

Miranda blows her nose.

Miranda	Maths.
Jim	I'll have a go at that.

He sits down next to her.

Miranda	Do you have to do it here?
Jim	I'll be as quiet as a mouse.

Miranda carries on with her work.

You got a bit of paper?

Miranda looks annoyed.

Eek, eek.

Despite herself, Miranda laughs.

Scene Two

The staffroom of St Xavier's. Mrs Pryme and Mr Cooper are sitting down.

Mrs Pryme takes a set of exercise books out of her bag and starts to mark them methodically.

Mr Cooper gets out a pile of exercise books, spills them on the floor and groans. He picks one up, opens it and tries to read it. He turns it upside down, then sideways, but still can't read it. He marks it.

Mr Cooper D−.

He picks up a handful of books and starts marking them very rapidly.

Simms, C+ ... Bashley, B ... Whitfield, A+ ... Walgrave, E please see me.

Mrs Pryme Harry?

Mr Cooper Yes, Janice?

Mrs Pryme Are you marking those without reading them first?

Mr Cooper I've had this lot for two years. I know what marks they get.

Mrs Pryme Don't you think that's a bit ...

Mr Cooper Don't worry. They don't take the slightest notice of what I write anyway.

The Head comes in. Mr Cooper hurriedly tidies up his spilt books.

Head Both of you teaching this afternoon?

Mrs Pryme and Mr Cooper reply hurriedly.

Mrs Pryme and Mr Cooper Yes.

Head Pity. I'm rather busy and I'm supposed to be taking 3G for history. I'd let them get on with some silent reading of their own, but that awful Jim McLindon's in the class.

Mrs Pryme Actually, Jim's work for me is improving.

The Head ignores her.

Head It was a mistake letting him join the school in the first place. What on earth do you do with a boy like that?

Act Two, Scene Three **47**

Mr Cooper Boil him in oil and serve him with chips.
Head What? That's not such a bad idea.
Mrs Pryme I think he is trying to make an effort, Mr Bryant.
Head A leopard can't change his spots, Janice.

The bell goes.

Oh well, I'll just have to try and hammer some facts into that thick head of his.

Scene Three

A classroom. Jim, Miranda and Peter come on with their books and bags.

Head Good afternoon, 3G.
All Good afternoon, Headmaster.
Head Your homework was to write about achievement in the twentieth century. I'll collect your work now.

Peter and Miranda hand in their homework. Jim is getting his exercise book out of his bag.

Head There's no use expecting homework from you, is there, McLindon?
Jim I've done it, Sir.
Head What's your excuse this time?
Jim I've done it.
Head You realise you'll have to complete the homework in detention anyway?
Jim It's here, Sir.
Head What?
Jim I spent three hours doing it last night.

The Head looks very suspicious.

Head Show me.

Jim opens his exercise book.

Head Copied out of a library book, I'll bet.

Jim   I did it myself.

Head   Then read some of it out. I can always tell when a pupil's copied something.

Jim   Do I have to?

Head   I wouldn't've asked you if you didn't. Stand up to read.

Reluctantly, Jim gets up.

Jim   It's about George Leigh Mallory, the mountaineer.

Head   Get on with it, McLindon. I'm sure we're all waiting for the words of wisdom to pour forth from your lips.

Peter sniggers sycophantically. Jim reads.

Jim   George Leigh Mallory is remembered as one of the greatest explorers which ever came from the British Isles . . .

Head   'Whoever', McLindon, not 'Which ever'.

Jim continues reading.

Jim   Above all else, he is remembered for his courageous attempt to be the first man to climb Mount Everest. When asked why he wanted to do it, he simply said, 'Because it's there.' This sets an example to all of us not to be afraid of trying to do things what seem impossible . . .

Peter   Like writing good English.

The Head reproves Peter.

Head   Peter.

Jim continues to read.

Jim   Whether he ever reached the top of the mountain, we'll never know. He was last seen eight hundred feet from the summit, climbing strongly with his companion, Sandy Irvine. Then cloud came down and they were hidden from view. They were never seen again and their bodies were never found.

The Head interrupts.

Head   It's certainly too badly written to have been copied. Give it here.

Jim hands in his book. The Head glances through it. Miranda whispers across to Jim.

Miranda It was good, Jim.

Jim whispers back, indicating the Head.

Jim I hate him.

Miranda whispers.

Miranda Never mind. Think about later. Mum and Dad are taking us ice-skating for a treat.

Jim forgets to whisper and bursts out.

Jim Ice-skating? Bloody hell!

Head McLindon!

Scene Four

We hear a loud burst of ice-arena music. The lights come up upon Mr and Mrs Welland, wearing skates and carrying spare pairs for Jim and Miranda.

While the children are putting their skates on, Mr and Mrs Welland start a Torvill and Dean style routine. The effect should be exaggerated and funny.

Miranda gets her skates on quickly and joins in. She is a skilled skater. Jim has much more trouble. He gets up and falls straight down.

Jim Help!

Mr and Mrs Welland pick him up and start taking him round the rink. They reduce their support for him and he starts to skate alone.

Slow at first, he quickly gets the hang of it and is putting in twirls and jumps. The others stop to watch. He finishes with a great leap and twirl. As he lands, the others applaud.

Am I good or what?

Jim slips over. The music stops and the lights fade to blackout.

Scene Five

The lights up on the alley and the bins. Stubby is bouncing a basketball from hand to hand. After a moment, Jim comes on, holding a letter.

Jim Hiya, Stubbs.
Stubby ignores him and carries on bouncing the ball.
What's the matter? Not talking?

Stubby It's not me not talking, is it?

Jim What's that supposed to mean?

Stubby Nothing.

Jim Look, I've been busy. I've had things to do.

Stubby We was meant to be going back to the quarry, remember?

Jim I haven't had time.

Stubby I told everyone I was going to climb it.

Jim We will.

Stubby Now Deano keeps getting on at me. 'Climbed Everest yet, Plastic Man?'

Jim We will do. Promise.

Stubby Today?

Jim Not today.
Stubby, disappointed, goes back to bouncing the ball.
I've got something to do today. I need your help.

Stubby What?
Jim holds out a letter.

Jim I want you to give this to my mum.

Stubby What is it?

Act Two, Scene Five

Jim Nothing. Just a letter. I saw her down the shops. She'll be back soon.

Stubby Give it her yourself.

Jim I don't want to. She doesn't take things right from me. Go on.

Stubby When're we going back to the quarry?

Jim This Saturday, honest.

Stubby All right.

He takes the letter.

Jim Look, here she is. Give it to her.

Jim dives out of sight as Sharon enters and goes to her back gate.

Stubby Mrs McLindon, Mrs McLindon!

Sharon What is it?

Stubby holds out the letter.

Stubby It's for you.

Sharon Who from?

Stubby Dunno. Someone just asked me to give it to you.

Sharon takes the letter and exits through the back gate. Stubby waits a minute, then signals Jim to come out.

Jim Did she take it?

Stubby nods.

Did she read it?

Stubby shrugs.

The lights go down on Jim and Stubby, who freeze, as Sharon is lit. She takes off her coat and starts to open her hairdressing carry-case. She decides she will read the letter. She takes it from her coat and starts to read.

Sharon Dear Mum,
This is just to say that I miss seeing you and think about you everyday.

Jim's voice is heard continuing.

Jim I can understand about you not wanting to see me. I know I've been very bad and a lot of trouble. I'm sorry about smashing that window.

I've tried being better since then. My teachers say I'm not as bad as I was.

I do love you, Mum. Please stay friends with me. Please still be my mum.
Love, Jim.

Sharon looks for a moment out of an imaginary window, down towards Jim. The lights come down on her and up on Jim and Stubby.

Jim Think she'll take any notice?

Stubby Search me.

Jim I want her to.

Stubby You can't tell. Not with mums. They're not like ordinary people.

Sharon comes on quickly, then pulls herself up.

Jim Mum?

Sharon takes a step towards him.

Mum?

Sharon holds out her arms. Jim runs into them and she hugs him. Matt comes out of the Takeaway with a bin bag.

Matt What's going off here then?

Sharon releases Jim.

I thought we had an agreement, Sharon.

Sharon We do.

Matt Then what you hugging him for? I let him off smashing my window – you don't see him again.

Sharon I know, Matt.

Matt An agreement's an agreement.

Sharon He just came round.

Matt I told you: I don't want lumbering with someone else's kid when we get married.

Jim is horrified.

Jim Mum?

Sharon I was going to tell you.

Jim You're marrying him?

Matt That's right. Next month, all right? And you aren't part of the picture, so get that straight in your head for starters.

Sharon Jim, it's the best thing for all of us. You'd feel out of place, especially when Matt and me start a family of our own. The Wellands'll bring you up better than I ever could. They've got all those books and paintings. I was going to tell you. It's for the best.

Sharon moves to put her arm round Jim again. He backs away. Stubby goes up to him.

Stubby Come on, let's go to my place.

Jim Get off! Get off all of you!

Jim runs off. Stubby looks at Sharon and Matt.

Scene Six

A fierce wind starts and the lights are brilliant white. Jim enters in the thick of the storm.

Jim I was so close. So close to the top of Chomolungma. Goddess Mother of the World. Eight hundred feet. Four hours walking. I could see the peak up above me. Every step I took, crunching into the treacherous snow, I imagined myself there – on top of the world. It had been a hard slog, the last few days, but early on June the eighth, I set out from Camp Six full of hope and determination. All the sweat, the pain was going to be worth it. The air was pitifully thin. It burned my lungs but I didn't mind. My legs and arms ached with exhaustion but it didn't matter any more. Everything I wanted in life was going to be mine. I could see it. I could see it.

And then the cloud came in. The blizzard started with blinding fine snow that cut into my eyes and mouth. I couldn't see anything any more. I was lost. Chomolungma wanted to destroy me.

Scene Seven

The school bell rings in the school playground. Jim sits down slowly on the ground. Miranda crosses behind him.

Miranda Come on, Jim, we'll be late for Maths.

No response from Jim.

Maths!

She goes off. Jim stays sitting. The Head comes on.

Head McLindon! What are you doing there?

Still no response from Jim.

McLindon!

No response.

Get up!

Jim gets up slowly.

Where are you meant to be now?

Jim I don't know.

Head Sir.

Jim responds lifelessly.

Jim Sir.

Head What on earth do you think you're playing at, hanging round here when you should be in class? Well? . . . I asked you a question, boy.

Jim I don't know . . . Sir.

Head Don't get clever with me, young man, or I'll get clever

	with you and, believe me, you'll come off the worse. Are you ill or something?
Jim	No.
Head	But you don't know which class you're supposed to be in?
Jim	No.
Head	Sir! I've had just about as much of your bad manners as I'm going to take, McLindon. I didn't think much of you when you came here and I've seen nothing since to make me change my mind. Mrs Pryme sticks up for you; she seems to think she's seen a change in you, but I'm afraid Mrs Pryme is rather too good-hearted. I'm different; I'm an old hand, McLindon, and I've seen it all before. You're no good, right the way through. You're no good at school and you're no good at home.
Jim	Sod off!
Head	What did you say?
Jim	You heard me.
Head	How dare you! How dare you address a teacher like that. I've a good mind to . . .
Jim	Oh sod off!
	Jim runs off. The Head looks after Jim, absolutely astonished. No one has ever spoken to him like that before.

Scene Eight

Lights up on the Wellands' kitchen. Mr Welland is on the phone. Mrs Welland is listening in.

Mr Welland	Yes . . . yes . . . Like I say, he's not at home at the moment, but the minute Jim comes in, I'll have a very serious talk with him. Yes, we'll come up and discuss his future at St Xavier's. Sorry about the trouble, Mr Bryant.

	He puts the phone down.
	I'll throttle Jim; I will, I'll throttle him.
Mrs Welland	Alan, calm down. We don't want it triggering you off.
	Mr and Mrs Welland exchange glances.
Mr Welland	He'll expel Jim, of course.
Mrs Welland	Do you think so?
	The front door opens offstage.
	That'll be the kids.
Mr Welland	Right. I'm going to sort that little tyke out once and for all.
Mrs Welland	I'll deal with it, Alan. You just keep quiet.
Mr Welland	If you don't sort it, I will.
	Miranda comes in. She is trying extra hard to be cheerful.
Miranda	Hiya.
Mrs Welland	Hello, love.
Mr Welland	Where's Jim?
Miranda	I think he's gone up to his room. What's for tea, Mum? Anything nice?
Mr Welland	What happened at school today?
Miranda	Oh nothing much. Mr Cooper fell asleep at choir practice, but there's nothing unusual about that.
Mrs Welland	What happened with Jim, love?
	Miranda responds innocently.
Miranda	Jim?
Mrs Welland	We've had the Headmaster on the phone.
Miranda	Oh, I think there was a little bit of trouble, but the Head gets on at everyone some time or other.
	Mr Welland goes to the door and calls upstairs.
Mr Welland	Jim . . . Jim!
Miranda	Dad, the Head always picks on Jim. He doesn't understand him. It's not Jim's fault.
Mr Welland	Jim! Get down here at once.

Act Two, Scene Eight

Mrs Welland addresses her husband.

Mrs Welland It won't do any good to have a go at him. He's had enough of being told off for one day.

Jim enters and stands in the doorway.

Mr Welland Come and sit down, Jim.

Miranda pleads with her father.

Miranda Dad.

Mrs Welland speaks to Jim.

Mrs Welland What happened this afternoon?

Jim Nothing.

Mr Welland Nothing!

Mrs Welland We've had the Headmaster on the phone for half an hour.

Mr Welland He wants you out of St Xavier's.

Jim Good. I don't want to stay there.

Mr Welland Stop being so stupid.

Mrs Welland Alan.

Mr Welland We all understand you've been through a hard time. We all wish you and your mother got on. But it's not an excuse for you to be completely bloody-minded for the rest of your life. You've got to think of other people, not just yourself.

Jim Why? I don't care what anyone thinks of me.

Mr Welland That's a downright stupid attitude to take.

Jim I might be stupid, but at least I'm not mad.

Slight pause while everyone takes in what Jim's said.

Mrs Welland Jim.

Mr Welland What do you mean by that?

Jim You are, aren't you? Mad.

Points to Miranda.

That's what she said.

Miranda You promised you'd never . . .

Jim You lock yourself away in your room for days with

	little paper fish. Say that you're working, but really you've gone mad. That's what she said.
Miranda	I didn't, Daddy, I didn't.
	She speaks to Jim.
	How could you? You promised!
Mrs Welland	I think you've said more than enough for one night, don't you, Jim? Go up to your room.
	Jim goes out defiantly. Miranda is mortified and close to tears.
Miranda	Daddy, I didn't say . . . I just wanted Jim to know . . . he felt so bad about his mum. I hate him! I hate him!
	Mrs Welland puts her arm round Miranda.
Mrs Welland	It's all right, Miri, it's all right.
Mr Welland	I'll get in touch with Tony first thing in the morning. That boy's not staying a moment longer.

Scene Nine

Moonlight on the kitchen. Jim creeps in with a torch. He takes a quick drink of milk from a carton, pulls on a jacket, then climbs out through the window.

As Jim walks downstage, we have the Everest poster lit and a central white light and wind: wilder than ever. Jim speaks from the front of the stage.

Jim A few hundred feet from the summit of Chomolungma and I'm beaten. I know I can never make it up there now. I could've turned back for Camp Six an hour or two ago and still have made it to safety before nightfall. But I didn't. I couldn't turn back. I kept slogging on through this hellish gale, knowing that I'd never get any higher. Every step I take could be my last. I can't see where I'm putting my feet. They keep slipping. I don't know what's to the side of me; most probably a drop of hundreds of feet – ice and rock below waiting to smash my body

Act Two, Scene Nine

to pulp. Night must come and with it, a cold that'll stop my heart beating and freeze my blood to ice. I know this and still I climb on. Because there's nothing for me down there. My whole life was a dream – the dream of climbing Chomolungma. It drove me on – made me wake up, day after day, excited to be living, preparing to make my dream come real . . . And now it's over. I can't breathe. My lungs are exhausted. There's no strength in my legs to lift my feet. The others, Odell, Somervell, none of them can help me now. They'll never know what happened. They'll say it was an accident. Bad luck. I slipped and fell to my death. They don't know what I feel inside now. My life is over before my body's died. None of them understands what the mountain means to me. It's everything.

Already it's getting dark. Colder. A cold I can feel inside each bone. I'm turning to ice. My breath is freezing on my lips. All there is left is black, winter night. And for me to walk into it.

A great howl of wind. The quarry appears and Jim walks to the foot of it.
We hear Stubby shouting over from offstage.

Stubby Jim! Jim! . . . Jim! . . . Jim!

Stubby runs on. The light and wind become normal.

I knew you'd be here. I knew it . . . Boy, are you in trouble. There's police out looking for you everywhere. The Wellands phoned them as soon as they found you were missing. Two of them came to our house. Huge great copper one of them. Mum nearly choked on her cornflakes.

Jim You didn't tell them about here?

Stubby Course not. Said I didn't see you much these days anyway. And I made sure they didn't follow me here. I doubled back down our alley in case they were following. What're you going to do?

Jim Nothing. Go away, Stubbs.

Stubby It's all right. I don't mind getting into trouble with you. They're bound to find us and then you're for it.

Jim No one knows about this place except you and Miranda. She won't tell them. She wants rid of me, same as the rest of them.

Stubby You're dead brave, running away. I want to an' all.

Jim starts climbing the quarry face. Stubby moves towards the foot of the quarry.

I won't tell anyone. I'll bring some food after school. We've got some tins of Spaghetti Hoops. We'll have to eat them cold . . . Jim?

Jim keeps on climbing. Stubby starts up the quarry face.

Jim!

Jim keeps climbing and turns around.

Jim Go away!

Stubby I'll run away with you. It'll be great. I'm sick of it round here. Everyone making fun.

Jim Go home, Stubbs.

Stubby Two's better than one. They'll never find us.

Jim I don't want anyone else with me.

Stubby I'll be whosit . . . Odell . . . I'll make all the camps, lay in the supplies.

Jim That was just a game, stupid.

Stubby Well, games are better than real life then. We'll be a team. We'll climb Everest.

Jim I don't want you with me.

Stubby Go on.

Jim No.

Stubby Let me stay.

Jim No.

Stubby You can't stop me coming up if I want to.

Jim Go home!

Stubby Why won't you let me?

Jim Because you're useless.
Stubby I won't go away.
Jim's voice turns nasty.
Jim Stubby, I don't want a plastic man with me.
Stubby is shattered. He looks disbelievingly up at Jim.
Stubby Jim?
Jim Go on. Clear off, Plastic Man.
Slowly Stubby moves away. He takes a last look at Jim, who turns away. Stubby goes off.
Jim climbs on and picks up the cardigan left by Miranda. He thinks about throwing it down, then throws it over his shoulder and climbs on a little way to a new ledge.

Scene Ten

The Wellands' kitchen. Mr Welland is on the phone. Tony, Miranda and Mrs Welland are listening.

Mr Welland No one's got any idea. Have you asked the other pupils in his class? Yes, of course. Well, if you hear anything. Thanks. Bye.
He puts the phone down.
Mrs Welland Nothing?
Mr Welland The damned Headmaster's delighted Jim's missing if you ask me.
Miranda That's typical of Mr Bryant.
Tony Jim didn't say anything last night? Didn't give any idea of where he'd go to?
Mrs Welland Tony, if he had, we'd've told you.
Tony You should've got in touch with me if you thought there were problems.
Mr Welland We were managing very well, thank you.
Tony You can't've managed that well, if Jim's done a

	runner. You've landed me right in it. I had to fight to get permission for him to be fostered.
Mrs Welland	Is that all you can think about? The poor boy might be in danger.
Mr Welland	Miranda, get off to school.
Miranda	Do I have to?
Mr Welland	Yes. You'll just be in the way here.
Tony	There's bound to be an enquiry.

Miranda speaks reluctantly.

| **Miranda** | Dad. |
| **Mrs Welland** | Where can he be? You tried his mother? |

Tony snaps back.

Tony	Of course I did.
Mrs Welland	I'm only asking.
Tony	Sorry. The police have looked everywhere. Miranda, do you know anywhere Jim liked going? Anywhere he might try and hide out?

There is a slight pause before Miranda answers.

| **Miranda** | No. |
| **Mr Welland** | Then where the hell is he? People don't just disappear, do they? |

Scene Eleven

The quarry. Jim is at the highest point. There is a brilliant white light, but no wind. Jim addresses the audience.

| **Jim** | This'll be the last place. On top of the world. |

Jim waves Miranda's cardigan slowly, like a flag. He wraps it over his shoulders.

I'll just wait. Wait for it all to finish. I'll sleep or something and it'll all stop.

Act Two, Scene Eleven

It's so cold. I can't feel anything. I can't feel pain anymore. Nothing. I'm frozen; as hard and cold as ice. Nothing matters. No one matters anymore. There's only me and a mountain that doesn't even know I'm here. Chomolungma.

He steps towards the edge and looks out into space. He is contemplating jumping. Miranda enters, but doesn't see him. She calls out.

Miranda Jim! . . . Jim!

No response from Jim. Miranda keeps looking, then sees him.

Jim! It's me.

No response.

Mallory! Mallory, can you hear me?

Jim looks vacantly towards her, but doesn't speak.

Mallory, I've come with the rescue party. When you disappeared, we all came looking for you. You're safe. Step back from the edge.

Jim Leave me alone.

Miranda Come down. We'll go back together. It'll be all right.

Jim Please leave me alone.

Miranda starts climbing the foot of the quarry. She pauses to find a safe foothold.

Miranda I can get so far, but you'll have to meet me halfway.

Jim Don't come up here. It's not safe.

Miranda climbs to the camp Stubby made.

It's not safe.

Miranda You got up.

Jim Stay there.

Miranda, short of breath, sits down in the camp. She picks up the chocolate Stubby stashed.

Miranda Look, I've found the pemmican we left. We can share it when I get to the top.

Jim You shouldn't be here.

Miranda	You can't climb mountains on your own.
Jim	I don't want you here.
Miranda	I know. I came because I wanted to.
Jim	Don't pretend you want to help me, because you don't. I gave away your secret. You hate me, don't you?
Miranda	Do you want me to?
Jim	Yes.
Miranda	You want everyone to hate you, don't you? Mum, Dad, all the teachers at school. Me.
Jim	Yes.
Miranda	That's why I won't.
	She stands up again.
Jim	Don't come up here.
Miranda	Did Mallory die on Everest?
Jim	Yeah, course he did.
Miranda	What killed him?
Jim	He was caught in a blizzard, most probably. Froze to death.
Miranda	He needn't have. He could've turned back.
Jim	No, he couldn't! He had to keep going. He had to try and climb Everest.
Miranda	But he must've known near the top he couldn't make it.
Jim	He couldn't come down. It was the only mountain in the world for him.
Miranda	Then it was the wrong mountain.
	She starts to climb higher.
Jim	You'll fall if you try and come up here. The rock's crumbly.
Miranda	Which way should I go?
Jim	Back down.
Miranda	I'm coming up one way or another.

Act Two, Scene Eleven

She starts to move again.

Jim To your left. There's a handhold there.

Miranda moves to the narrow ledge and looks down.

Miranda Oooh . . . I don't like heights.

Jim Don't look down. You'll get giddy.

Miranda looks nervous about falling.

Miranda You know what I always wanted, Jim? I always wanted a brother. To do things like this with.

Jim You're crazy.

Miranda I love Mum and Dad, but sometimes it's so lonely at home. 'Cos I'm a girl, they don't let me do anything exciting. They think girls break easily or something.

Jim Watch your feet!

Miranda Mum and Dad said they'd tried, but they couldn't. It's funny; I don't like boys much, but it had to be brother. I always wanted a brother who'd call me 'sis'. Isn't that stupid? 'Sis'? That's why I didn't mind you coming. Didn't know what we were letting ourselves in for.

She starts moving again.

Jim Don't try coming across!

Miranda I'm halfway there.

Jim It's too dangerous.

Miranda It's as dangerous to go back.

She takes another step. Part of the quarry gives way and she slips. She clutches at a tenuous handhold and dangles. It's clear she can't hold on for long.

Help! Help me!

Jim moves towards her.

Jim Hang on.

Miranda I can't.

Jim Hang on!

Miranda I'm slipping.

Jim inches towards her.

Jim Give me your hand.

Miranda I can't.

Jim Come on.

Miranda I can't let go.

Jim inches closer, holding out his hand.

Jim Come on. You're all right.

Miranda holds out her hand. As Jim takes hold of it, more of the rockface gives way. Jim manages to hold on and she scrambles back up. They find safe footholds and take a couple of moments to calm down. They look at each other.

Jim You dropped the chocolate then?

Miranda nods. Slight pause.

Miranda I'd've been dead if you hadn't grabbed me.

Jim You shouldn't've come up.

Miranda Thanks very much.

Jim No, but . . . well . . . thanks. We can climb up onto the top. I'll take you home.

Miranda is extremely frightened.

Miranda I'm not moving another step.

Jim It's only a bit further and it's not too slippy.

Miranda I'm not moving!

Jim I'll go up on the top. Go for help.

Miranda grabs his arm.

Miranda You're not going anywhere.

Jim It won't take long.

Miranda You are not leaving me here alone. All right?

Jim All right . . . So what are we going to do?

Miranda I don't know.

Jim Better not try tap dancing, eh?

Miranda   Jim, I'm scared.

Jim   Me too, sis.

They hold hands for comfort. They start to cry for help.

Scene Twelve

The Wellands' kitchen.

Mr Welland   Thank God for you, Stubby. Telling the police where Jim was hiding.

Stubby   He'll kill me.

Tony   I don't think so.

Mr Welland   From the look on his face when they finally brought him and Miri back up, I think he might actually have learned something today.

Stubby   It must've been dead good fun getting winched up.

Tony   They were scared out of their wits, Stubby.

Stubby   What'll happen to Jim?

Mr Welland   Nothing much. I think he's had enough of a scare to keep him out of mischief for a while.

Tony   We'll make arrangements for him to go back to the children's home first thing tomorrow.

Mr Welland   Don't you dare. After all the trouble Miri went to finding him, I think he's with us for good.

Miranda comes on, wiping her hair with a towel.

Miranda   Stubby, you're a hero!

Stubby   Am I?

Miranda   Absolutely.

Stubby   Jim didn't mind me going to the coppers?

Miranda   He thinks you're brilliant.

Mrs Welland comes on with Jim, who is looking the smartest we've ever seen him. He's carrying the poster of Everest.

Mrs Welland You're staying for supper, aren't you, Stubby?

Stubby looks worried about Jim's reaction.

Stubby I don't know.

Jim You've got to. It's chocolate mousse.

Stubby Oh, right.

Mrs Welland Sit down everybody, then I can serve up.

Jim Yeah, in a minute. I gotta do something first.

Jim walks into the neutral space, which is now the back garden.

Mr Welland Miri, keep an eye on him.

Miranda goes to look. Jim is unrolling the poster and putting a vertical crease in it to keep it open. Miranda indicates to the others to come out and join them. Jim looks back over his shoulder at them.

Jim What it is . . . is . . . I want to say . . . because I was rotten to Stubby. I said things . . . And to you, Mr Welland. I'm sorry what I said.

Mr Welland I didn't hear him say anything, did you, Stubby?

Stubby No.

Jim Yeah but . . . Like I've been and the way you've been.

Miranda Jim, do shut up so we can get on with our dinner.

Jim All right, sis. Wrong mountain, that's all.

He sets fire to the poster. As it burns, the lights fade.

The end.

Mariza's Story

Michele Celeste

List of Characters

Mariza	Eight years old
Mum	Mariza's mother
Tania	Mariza's sister, twelve years old
Anita	Nine years old
Carrot	Eight years old
Rambo	Thirteen years old
Marcelo	Nine years old
Cop	
Old woman	
Figure/Teacher	
Anita's mum	
Anita's dad	
Baker	

Various men, women, passers-by, thieves, drivers, streetkids and other children.

Time and place

The present. The play takes place on the background of the current massacre of streetchildren specifically in Brazil. However, the mistreatment and persecution of streetchildren are of global proportions (Colombia, Guatemala, Philippines, Mexico, India, Bangladesh, Iraq, Turkey, USA and some African countries).

ACT ONE

Scene One

Mariza, eight years old, her Mum, in her thirties, and her sister Tania, twelve, walking at night along a road. Traffic goes past. They have been walking for hours. Mum and Tania carry sacks on their heads. Mariza falls behind.

She is wearing an old coat and has a battered doll in her hand.

Very tired, they stop and put down their loads.

They are dusty and dressed in old clothes and have bare feet.

Tania sits on the sack, soon imitated by Mariza who sits on her Mum's sack.

Tania Mum, look! The bus.

Mum We don't have money for tickets.

Mariza goes towards the bus.

Mariza!

Tania Get back here!

They carry on walking. Again, they stop even more tired than before.

Mum It's a long way to go home.

Tania Another four miles.

Mariza Another four miles.

Tania You shut up.

Mum Come on, let's try.

Tania Mum, wait.

Tania tries hailing cars, without any luck.

With so many cars going by . . . with so many lorries and buses . . . why can't we take one.

Mum	I told you, Tania, we haven't got the money for the tickets.
Tania	Aren't people kind?
Mum	Not to those like us.
Tania	We are people like everybody else, aren't we?
Mum	I know, Tania. But we are not like them.
Mariza	Why aren't we like people with cars, Mum?
Mum	We're street people. They're car people. Come on. Let's try to cover another stretch. I'm worried about our home.

They walk again, Mariza losing ground. Her Mum sees her and stops.

Tania	Don't stop now.
Mum	Tania. Mariza's too small to walk for so long.
Tania	She's too heavy to be carried.

Mum ties a rope round Mariza's waist.

Mum	I don't want to lose you. It's a dark night.

Tania tries flagging more cars. Again without any luck.

Mum	Come on, let's walk on.
Tania	But it's too far!
Mum	We have done this road yesterday. And the day before, and before . . . To town and back.
Tania	How comes tonight we can't do it?

Mariza starts crying.

Mum	She's hungry.
Tania	We haven't eaten anything today, have we?
Mum	Yes, it's harder tonight. We have eaten less and less each day.
Tania	Yes, but today nothing at all.

Tania puts her load down.

I can't do it, Mum. I'd rather die here.

Mum	Look, Tania, rest a bit here with your little sister. I'll

Act One, Scene One

walk on, on my own. It's important I get home. We left it this morning with nobody looking after it. There's so many thieves about. You can't leave your house on its own any longer. Our house is all we have.

Tania Go ahead then.

Mum hands the end of the rope to Tania.

Mum Make your way a little at a time. Watch yourself from strangers.

Tania Yes, Mum.

Mum walks away. Mariza cries. Tania calms her. Then Tania and Mariza resume walking. Mariza stops.

Come on.

Mariza It's dark.

Tania It's night, that's why.

Mariza It gets darker, Tania.

Tania It's your eyes, Mariza. Please, don't fall asleep.

Mariza collapses. Tania speaks angrily to herself.

Oh, how can we walk like this! We must get home. Ah! Maybe if they see a child, one of the cars'll stop.

Tania holds Mariza in front of her as she tries to stop the passing traffic. Then, the braking noise of a car is heard.

Oh! It's stopped! We're lucky, Mariza!

The Driver comes up to them and looks them up and down.

Driver Are you going to the favela?

Tania Yes! Please, Senhor! Gives us a lift.

The Driver continues to look at them. Mariza, very drowsy, sits on Tania's sack.

It's four miles away. We've been walking all day! Your car won't take five minutes.

Driver How old are you?

Tania	I'm twelve.
Driver	And.
Tania	My sister. She's only eight.
Driver	I give you a lift, come on. But leave your sister here.
Tania	Why?
Driver	I'll come back for her later.
Tania	But it won't cost you anything to carry both of us.
Driver	See there? My car is already full. I can only take one person more.
Tania	She'll sit on my lap.
Driver	I'll take you first, then I'll come and get the child.
Tania	I don't believe you.
Driver	I'll give you some money as well.

Tania answers suspiciously.

Tania	Money?
Driver	I'll come later to fetch her.
Tania	I can't leave my sister.
Driver	Tell her to wait there. Until I'm back.
Tania	Mariza'll be scared on her own.
Driver	She's fallen asleep.
Tania	We have not eaten all day.
Driver	Let her sleep there until I'm back. It won't take more than ten minutes. I'll give you money.
Tania	Mum has earned very little today. We couldn't even pay the bus. Why don't you want to take her? You have no heart.
Driver	It's up to you.
Tania	No, I'd rather walk.
Driver	How can you carry her with your load?
Tania	That's my business.
Driver	Good luck then.

The Driver starts to go.

Tania No! You've been the only one kind enough to stop. Maybe, maybe. Yes! I can tie up my sister. So if she wakes up she won't wander off.

She ties the sleeping Mariza to a post. The Driver offers her some money.

Driver Here.

Tania takes the money and looks at it. She is amazed that it is so much.

Tania Then you'll come for her? In ten minutes?
Driver Of course I will.

She follows the Driver off. Noise of the car starting and leaving.

Scene Two

A favela. One or two thieves are looting a shack of its possessions.

Mum comes on. She sees the thieves and screams. The thieves run off.

Mum Oh, my home! My home! They stole everything in it! Who can be so cruel to wreck a poor woman's shack! Who can be so cruel to steal from those who have nothing! Who can do this, to a mother who walks to town and back every day.

Oh, God, why didn't you stop the wreckers! Why didn't God strike the thieves with his lightning? Poor, desperate people stole my shack so they can build their own shack! This is what misery does to people!

She cries.

I rushed here to make sure this wouldn't happen! I was too late. Too late. It didn't stop the rain. It didn't protect us from the wind and the dust. Only a room with four planks and cardboard walls. But it was home. I have no strength left. I cannot even run back to my daughters to tell them not to walk anymore, not to struggle with each step! There's no home anymore waiting for you, my daughters!

She sobs and gathers the remains of her possessions around her.

Scene Three

The road where Mariza is. She wakes up.

Mariza Mum? Tania? Mum? Tania?

She stumbles around until the rope stops her.

Mum. Tania. Mum.

She cries and struggles with the rope. Eventually she manages to free herself and wanders off uncertainly.

Mum. Tania. Mum.

Scene Four

The road. Mum walks wearily on.

Mum Tania? Mariza? Tania? They're not here. It's here where I left them. No, maybe it's further on. What if I've passed them without realising?
I told them not to stray away from this side of the road. Where are they?

She calls out.

Tania! Mariza!

She sees the rope on the ground.

Oh, no, God. I have already lost my poor house. I have already been robbed of all I had. Not my daughters as well, not my daughters. Tania! Mariza!

She tries to flag down the traffic without any luck.

Nobody stops to help me. What's happened to my daughters? Oh God, let me find them. Oh, God. Where are they? Who can help me now?

Mum wanders off looking for Mariza and Tania.

Scene Five

The noise of a car approaching and braking. The Driver pushes out Tania who is crying and bruised.

Driver Here you are! Go back to your little sister!
The Driver leaves.

Tania You're a bad, evil man! Mariza? Mariza?
She sees the rope.
Oh, no. Mariza! They have stolen her! Or a car has run her over! What's happened to her? What will I tell Mum! She told me to look after Mariza.
She exits calling out.
Mariza! Mariza!

Scene Six

Mariza comes on clutching her battered doll. Then Mum and then Tania wander in. They are unable to see each other. They call each other's names but they can't hear each other, as the way they call out and move, indicates they are a long way from each other. Calling and moving, they exit in different directions.

Scene Seven

Day. The Policeman comes on, on the beat. Then Mum.

Mum Senhor Officer.

The Policeman looks down at her.

Please help me.

Cop What is it?

Mum I've lost both my daughters.

Cop You 'lost' them?

Mum Yes! Last night, while walking home from town. One is Mariza. She's eight years old and the other is Tania, she is twelve.

Cop What you want me to do about that?

Mum Help me find them, please.

The Cop replies scornfully.

Cop Kids who run away to live on the streets.

Mum My daughters haven't run away! I lost them!

Cop There're thousands of children living on the streets. I can't help you there.

Mum Someone must help me. They're all I've got.

Cop You should have looked after them properly.

Mum How could I look after them properly? I had to get home because I was afraid of thieves and hooligans. I left my daughters to rest by the road and . . . and when I went back they weren't there anymore.

Cop You shouldn't have left them on their own, should you?

Mum But, I just explained why.

Cop Shut up. Move on.

Mum Help me, please.

Cop I said I can't help you! These streetkids are all thieves! As far as I'm concerned they're pests! They might be dead by now.

Mum Oh, God, no.

Cop Now, just go.

Mum Oh, my God.

Cop Move on. Move on.

Scene Eight

Day. The city. Mariza comes on and walks through the city. By now completely lost, she picks up rubbish from a bin to eat. She finds an unfinished can of Coke from the bin and drinks from it. Then, behind Mariza, a discarded fridge cardboard box takes on life. It stealthily moves towards her with unfriendly intentions. At the last moment, Mariza hears it and turns. She screams and back away. The box corners her.

Mariza, as a last resort, holds out her can of drink. A hand comes out of the box and grabs it. Noisy drinking from inside. The can is tossed out. Marcelo, inside the box, speaks in a strange voice.

Marcelo I'm sorry. I didn't realise you were thirsty.

He speaks accusingly.

Another runaway! Oh-oh!

Mariza is scared.

What are you doing in a big city like this?

Mariza I . . . I . . . I'm looking for my mum.

Marcelo Looking for your mum, eh?

Mariza And my sister, Tania.

Marcelo I have heard all sorts of excuses from you lot.

Mariza It's true!

Marcelo Where do you think you'll find your mum and sister then?

Mariza shrugs. There is a pause.

Where!

Mariza I . . . I don't know.

Marcelo You're a runaway!

Mariza No . . . I'm not a runaway.

Marcelo Have you seen how many children are living on the streets here?

Mariza I . . . I've just got here.
Marcelo Ah-ha! The street is no place for a little girl.
Mariza I'm only looking for . . .

Marcelo cuts in.

Marcelo Be warned! If a cop nicks you, he'll send you into an orphanage, where they beat you all the time! Aren't you scared now?

Mariza nods. There is a pause.

Why don't you go back home?

Mariza Home? Which way's my home?
Marcelo Oh, yes, go on pretending you're lost. Dirty clothes, broken shoes. There you are. Good advice is lost on urchins like you.

The box makes an attempt to grab Mariza.

Mariza Aaaahhhhh!

Mariza drops her coat and runs off. Marcelo, a street kid, comes out of the box and laughs.

Marcelo Ha! Ha! Ha! What do I see there? Another kid, newcomer to the city. Ha! Ha! Ha! I'll give him a fright too. Ha! Ha! Ha!

He gets back into the box and exits laughing.

Scene Nine

Mum looking for Mariza in the city. She finds Mariza's coat on the ground and picks it up. With renewed hope, she exits looking for her daughters.

Scene Ten

Night. A shocked and very tired Mariza comes on, scared of all those immense buildings and not a human being in sight. She stumbles into someone

Act One, Scene Ten

sleeping on the pavement, totally enveloped in a blanket on a cardboard sheet. She rushes away scared. But the sleeper has not moved. Not seeing any other human being around, hesitantly, she goes back and peeps under the blanket trying to see the face of the sleeper, believing to have caught a glimpse of her mum.

Mariza Mum? Mum?

Old Woman What?

Mariza Are you my mum?

An Old Woman who lives on the streets, emerges from the blanket, and mutters to herself.

Old Woman Waking me up in the middle of the night.

Mariza Are you my mum?

Old Woman Your mum!? I never had a child in my life! I'm not like some who call themselves mothers and then abandon their children on the street!

Mariza You are too old.

Old Woman You bet I am! I'm too old.

Mariza When I first saw you, I thought you were my mum.

Old Woman I'm not your mum!

Mariza I saw you sleeping like my mum.

Old Woman Oh.

Mariza Can you help me?

Old Woman How can I help you?

Mariza To find my mum?

Old Woman Where do you come from?

Mariza I come from?

Old Woman Can't you remember?

Mariza Brazil.

Old Woman Brazil? That's a large place.

Mariza You know where it is?

Old Woman	We are in Brazil! Everywhere you go in this country is Brazil!
Mariza	Where can I find my mum, then?
Old Woman	Brazil is a country! Like, like, ehm, like . . .
	She is at a loss.
	Ah! Like Spain! Portugal. England. It's a large place. Now you must tell me the place where your mum lives, the town, the street name and the number of the house.
Mariza	I think I come from . . . Medina?
Old Woman	I don't know where is this Mellina.
Mariza	Not Mellina. Me . . . rina!
Old Woman	Marina?
Mariza	Not Marina. Mellina!
Old Woman	Oh, Medina!
Mariza	Marina!
Old Woman	Messina!
Mariza	Messiah!
Old Woman	Messiah?!
	They are both totally confused.
Mariza	It is what I said the first time. Now I don't remember anymore.
Old Woman	Ask a policeman.
Mariza	If a policeman finds me, he'll send me to a orphanage!
Old Woman	Write the name then, where you come from on the cardboard.
	Mariza takes a felt pen and tries, but as she cannot write, draws a woman without a head.
	What does it say?
Mariza	This is my mum.
Old Woman	Oh, I can't see very well.
Mariza	I only went a year to school.

Old Woman	I never went to school at all. So, this is your mum's name?
Mariza	Yes.
Old Woman	Oh, I see. Looks like a drawing to me. My eyes. Well, I'm sorry I don't know. You woke me up in the middle of my sleep! I can't sleep well and you woke me up when I was sleeping so well . . . dreaming.

The Old Woman prepares to sleep again. Mariza, who is very tired, starts to go. But where? She stops and goes back.

Mariza	Can I sleep here?
Old Woman	Sleep here?
Mariza	I'm very tired.
Old Woman	Do what you like. Just don't wake me up.

The Old Woman goes to sleep. Mariza sleeps by her.

Scene Eleven

Day. Two streetkids, Anita and Marcelo, come on, begging. Mum comes on, still looking for her daughters. She carries Mariza's coat with her. Marcelo goes to beg from her, but seeing her condition, withdraws.

Mum	Excuse me. I'm looking for two girls. One is Tania, she is twelve and Mariza, she's eight. Have you seen them?

The two look at Mum and ignore her.

They're my daughters. One of them, the small one, you must be her age, had a doll with her.

Anita	We know nothing.
Mum	Please help me to find my daughters.
Marcelo	Just push off, will you?

Marcelo hides one arm as though it were missing. Anita hides a leg so to appear one legged. They resume begging. Looking at them, Mum starts begging as well.

Mum Give some money for my child. Give some money for my child. Give some money for my children.

Marcelo and Anita angrily approach Mum.

Anita You have no children!

Marcelo It's just an excuse.

Mum What you saying! I've lost my two daughters.

Anita You say that so the passersby give you money.

Marcelo You have to do better than that for begging!

Mum I need food like you.

Anita This is our pitch!

Mum Leave me alone!

Marcelo Go away!

Mum Kids like you should respect a mother! I've lost two daughters! I've to beg, to keep myself, while I look for them.

Anita pulls the coat from her and throws it away. Mum rushes to get it back.

Marcelo If you come back here, we'll bust you.

Anita Get lost!

They both drive Mum away.

Scene Twelve

The Old Woman and Mariza come on. The Old Woman pauses, then speaks suddenly.

Old Woman Go! Get me a glass of water.

Mariza From where?

Old Woman I don't know.

Act One, Scene Twelve

Mariza Oh.

Old Woman Get me some water!

Mariza Where?

Old Woman Steal it!

Mariza Steal it?!

Old Woman From the shop there. They sell mineral water.

Mariza What if they . . . ?

Old Woman Do what I tell you!

Mariza Yes, Mum.

Old Woman And don't call me Mum! Get on with it!

Mariza exits towards the shop.

Ah! What a hard life! At my age! But what can I do? I was left in the streets. I must have been five or six. I went playing with my friends and when I went back home it was shut. I waited long time for my parents to come back but they never came. What a hard life.

Mariza rushes in with a bottle of mineral water. The Old Woman drinks. She notices a Baker who comes on with a counter and places on it a loaf of bread and a cake. Customers come and go.

Now. I'm feeling peckish. It's usual with me. Everyday at breakfast time, I feel peckish. I fancy one of those, ehm, those . . . fancy looking South American cakes . . . for my breakfast.

She speaks to Mariza.

Go and get the cake!

Mariza They won't give it to me without money!

Old Woman Go and steal it! Make sure they don't see you! Or I'll kill you, little scamp!

Mariza If they see me, they'll beat me!

Old Woman Right. I'll do it myself then. Is that what you want, isn't it? The very old have to work while the very young only want to play.

She pretends she is going.

And then I won't need you anymore! And I'll leave you.

Mariza is very scared.

Mariza No, don't leave me.

Old Woman Oh, yes, I will. I'll leave you on your own, like your mum. Because you are a bad girl.

Mariza No.

Old Woman Okay. But you go and get the cake for your mummy. Go on.

Mariza Yes, Mum.

Mariza goes towards the Baker. A Policeman enters the bakery and starts talking indistinctly with the Baker.

Mariza gets to the shop and stealthily but surely closes in on the cake.

But as she is going for it, out of nowhere, Anita snatches the loaf of bread.

Anita runs off. The Baker and the Policeman make an attempt to pursue her. The Old Woman encourages Mariza to take advantage of the confusion, and steal the cake. She takes the cake to the Old Woman.

The Policeman gestures to the Baker to leave Anita to him and runs off after her.

The Baker gets back to his bakery. He is shocked to see the missing cake.

Old Woman Well done.

The Old Woman eats ravenously and drinks from the mineral water bottle.

It's nice to start the day with a little breakfast.

The Old Woman is left with only the last bit.

Oh, I just can't stuff anymore down.

She gives Mariza the remaining bit. Mariza eats.

Oh, my poor legs. I can't even stand and beg anymore. Come on, beg for me. People have more

Act One, Scene Twelve

pity of a child than an old woman. Isn't this a nasty world we're living in?

The Old Woman sits down. Mariza begs. Anita runs in and off again, followed by the Policeman who is after her. The Old Woman rebukes Mariza.

You must go up to people! Come on! You call that begging!

Mariza continues begging.

Mariza Senhor, please . . . Senhora . . . Only a cruzado.

The Old Woman whispers.

Old Woman No! Are you trying to save them money or something? Ask for ten cruzados!

Mariza Senhor, please ten cruzados . . . Senhora.

Anita runs in laughing, having lost the Cop and runs off again.

Old Woman If you don't make money you won't eat.

Mariza I'll try harder.

Old Woman You better. Or I'll leave you.

Mariza begs again with renewed effort. Again Anita runs in, pauses for breath, at last sure that she has lost the Cop behind her. She is going to bite the bread. Suddenly there is a gunshot from offstage. Anita falls down. Mariza rushes to her.

Leave her! Leave her! Don't meddle in other people's business.

Anita can't get up for the wound in her leg. Mariza helps her up. Anita limps off. Then the Cop enters holding Anita. Mariza, not sure whether the Cop has seen her helping Anita, runs to hide behind the Old Woman. The Old Woman looks at the loaf on the ground, wishing for the Cop to go away quickly. The Cop starts to go, but then he goes back to pick up the loaf and exits.

Damn!

Mariza resumes begging. A Man passerby is going to give her a coin when he notices her hand.

Man AAaaaaahhh!

He rushes off. Mariza looks at her hand.

Mariza It's blood. When I helped the kid up.

The Old Woman hits her with the stick.

Old Woman I told you don't interfere! You can't beg with blood on your hand! You have lost me money!

Mariza takes the beatings. Suddenly, seeing the Cop coming, the Old Woman pretends to nurse Mariza. The Cop comes on and sees them.

Cop Who is this child?

Old Woman She's my daughter, ehm.

Cop A daughter so young? At your old age?

Old Woman Ehm . . . You didn't let me finish, Officer. She's my daughter's daughter. I'm her granny. Let's be clear about this.

Cop I have never seen you with a child before.

Old Woman I've not been clear enough, have I?

Cop She's another runaway, isn't she?

Old Woman I'm her granny.

Cop You're using her for begging, aren't you?

Old Woman Look, my daughter, her mum, has died and I'm looking after her. Aren't I, lovey?

Cop I'm going to slam both of you in an orphanage.

Old Woman At my age?

Cop What you think, eh? No one is too old for punishment. Or too young.

Old Woman The girl would be begging, anyway.

Cop Right, you know the score, don't you?

Old Woman I do. I do. You'll get half of what she begs.

She gives him some money.

This is from yesterday.

The Cop pockets the money and exits.

You see, I could have said you were a runaway and you'd be you know where?

Mariza Yes, in an orphanage. A place where they keep children without parents. And they beat them up all the time in there. Are you an orphan as well?

Old Woman Well, yes. I was abandoned, that's orphan enough. I don't mind now. At my age everybody is an orphan. But it was not very good when I was small like you. Ehm, from now on, you better say I am your 'granny'.

Mariza But I want a mum.

Old Woman Well, I cannot be your mum! I'm too old for that sort of – of – of thing. Oh, I see, perhaps a granny is not good enough for you! Well, take it or leave it! You are afraid I leave you alone, aren't you? Like your mum and sister did.

There is a pause.

What a lovely sun. Come on. Get me a cardboard box, so I can sleep. Do it for granny.

Mariza No!

She starts to leave.

I only obey my mum.

Old Woman Come back here! I'll beat you!

Mariza You can't catch me!

Old Woman Come back!

Mariza A granny is too old to run.

Mariza runs off. The Old Woman tries to catch her.

Scene Thirteen

Another part of the city. Mariza sees a figure standing in the distance, with its back to her. The figure has a rolled up thing, like a carpet, under its arm. In a dark coat, a cane, like a blind person's, and dark glasses, the figure has a rather sinister appearance. Mariza looks with curiosity. Then the figure turns and seeing her starts walking towards her. Mariza runs away. The figure quickens its step after her.

Scene Fourteen

Another part of the city. Anita is scavenging from a rubbish bin. Marcelo comes on and joins her. They eat what they find. Anita finds two tins.

Anita   Beans.

Marcelo   Beans!

Anita   I've never been as lucky as this!

Marcelo   What's this?

Mariza is discovered buried in rubbish bags behind the bin. She is wearing a cap.

Anita   Hey, look! There's someone here!

Marcelo   A kid.

Anita   They killed another kid.

Marcelo   Leave her. It's the police and the killers paid by the shopowners to get rid of kids. Are we going to tell someone?

Anita   No, nobody cares.

They start leaving. Mariza moans from the rubbish and they stop.

Anita   What was that?

Marcelo   Nothing.

They start to leave again. There is another moan.

It must be her.

Anita   I didn't hear anything.

There is another moan. They rush to the rubbish.

Marcelo   She's alive.

Act One, Scene Fourteen

Anita I know her.

Marcelo I never seen her before.

Anita She was hanging out with the Old Woman. Helped me when the police were after me, for stealing the bread.

Marcelo Hey? What are you doing here?

Mariza I don't know.

Anita You're sleeping here.

Marcelo This is our rubbish! You're not supposed to sleep here.

Anita She's all bruised.

Marcelo She's got a beating from someone.

Anita You shouldn't have left the old woman.

Mariza I'm looking for my mum.

Marcelo Your mum? Ha! Ha! Ha!

Anita Who beat you up?

Mariza I don't know. A man. He followed me and then beat me up.

Anita She doesn't belong to a gang. You don't belong to a gang?

Mariza No.

Anita If you don't belong to a gang they'll always beat you up. With a gang nobody dares touch you.

Mariza I want to go home.

Marcelo Ha! Ha! Ha!

Anita Where's your home?

Mariza I don't know anymore.

Anita Look, you better join the gang here. If you join the gang, nobody will beat you up. We all look after each other. But we must obey him.

Rambo, the gang leader, enters with a streetkid. Anita speaks to Rambo.

She hasn't got a gang.

Marcelo	She's a softie.
Anita	We could try her.
	Rambo takes Mariza's cap. Mariza is afraid.
Rambo	I'll keep this. Can you fight?
	Mariza doesn't answer.
	She's no good for a gang.
Anita	I could teach her, Rambo.
Marcelo	She was hanging out with the Old Woman.
Rambo	Ha! Ha! Ha!
Streetkid	She's looking for mummy.
Rambo	She's no good.
Anita	She can steal.
Rambo	Can you steal?
	Anita gestures Mariza to say yes. Mariza nods.
	Well, as long as you can steal.
Mariza	I used to steal for the Old Woman. I can work as well.
Rambo	Work?
Mariza	Yes. Me and my sister helped my mum to sell flowers.
Rambo	All right. As long as you're not a parasite. You'll work. Doing what?
	Mariza shrugs. Anita butts in.
Anita	She can shoeshine.
	Anita winks at Mariza.
Mariza	Yes, I can shoeshine.
Rambo	Okay. You'll get a shoeshine kit. We'll see how you manage.
Mariza	Thanks for helping me, Anita.
Anita	You helped me first, when the cop wanted to kill me for the bread.
	They all follow Rambo off.

Scene Fifteen

Another day. A street. Mariza comes on with a shoeshine kit. She soon finds a customer and concentrates on her work while the Man reads a paper. A well-dressed Lady rushes on.

Lady Oh, damn!

She hops to Mariza. The Man is visibly impressed by the very attractive Lady.

I just stepped on a dog's mess! I have this wedding to go to! Do you mind if . . . It's my wedding!

The Man, with only one shoe cleaned, promptly obliges. Mariza, also struck by the Lady's looks, changes brush and starts shoeshining her shoe. The Lady gives her a coin. There's a brief intense moment as the two look at each other. The Lady shakes herself up and is walking away.

Mariza Excuse me.

Lady Yes.

Mariza What's your name?

Lady My name? Why?

Mariza You are not my mum, are you?

Lady Your mum? Me? Goodness, no.

Mariza shows her the coin.

Mariza My first coin. You look very nice.

Lady Oh. What's happened to your mum?

Mariza shrugs, smoothing the coin.

Mariza My mum was good to me.

Lady Well, I'm sorry.

The Lady goes. The Man waves to her. Mariza almost follows the Lady.

Mariza Mum?

Man Hey? You brat! One shoe yes, one shoe no!

Mariza rushes back to the shoeshine.

Just do your work. Don't hassle your customers.

Mariza I thought she was my mum.

Man Ha! Ha! Ha!

Mariza My mum was just like that. Well dressed and beautiful, very beautiful. My mum had a lot of money.

Man Ha! Ha! Ha!

He gives her a coin and goes. Puzzled, Mariza looks after him. Then she fondles the coin. As she is so occupied, Rambo and Marcelo come on unseen. Rambo gestures Marcelo to steal Mariza's shoeshine kit. Marcelo furtively does so and runs off. Mariza turns and sees no kit there. She looks about for it in great anxiety and exits doing so.

Scene Sixteen

Rambo comes on and waits, followed by Anita with the distressed Mariza. Mariza stops, afraid of Rambo. Anita convinces her to go to Rambo. Head bowed, Mariza does so, expecting punishment.

Rambo Where's the money?

Mariza gives him the two coins.

Is this all?

Mariza I couldn't earn anymore. Someone stole my kit.

Rambo They stole your kit? Well, if you let your kit be stolen, then you're not good enough. You can't stay in the gang.

Mariza I didn't know people would steal my kit.

Rambo It was your kit and you had to look after it! Until you paid me back for it.

Mariza Please, Rambo.

Act One, Scene Sixteen

Rambo I warned you! This is not a gang for softies! We can't have people like you who get their kit stolen.

Mariza If you throw me out of the gang. I'll be on my own. People'll beat me and do nasty things to me.

Rambo So much the worse for you.

Anita Rambo, she can do another job.

She adds apologetically.

Maybe.

Rambo No way.

Mariza Please.

Rambo Go away! Don't show your face to me until you've got the kit back. Okay?

Rambo goes. Mariza cries.

Anita Listen, Mariza. Crying is no good. You have to go and steal someone else's kit.

Mariza I can't.

Anita You must. That's what Rambo does with everybody. He himself sent someone to steal your kit, to test if you were sharp! It was to test you.

Mariza That's nasty.

Anita Well, if you go to another gang they'll test you just the same, you know? Every gang tests its members. If now you don't steal your kit back you'll be thrown out of the gang.

Mariza I only want my mum!

There is a pause.

Anita That's very soft.

Mariza Don't you want your mum?

Anita I ran away from her.

Mariza You ran away from your mum!?

Anita Mum was always fighting with my dad, she never stopped, and she never cared for me. She has no time for me.

Mariza My mum is not like that.

There is a pause. The mysterious figure comes on again. They see it and keep a wary eye on it.

My mum loves me. And she is beautiful and well dressed.

Anita Why she's left you then?

Mariza I don't know.

Anita Your mum doesn't love you, that's why!

Mariza Mum does love me! She does! She's so beautiful . . . my mum. Like a film star.

Anita Why doesn't she come and get you then?

Mariza I don't know.

The figure starts to walk towards them. They run off. The figure exits after them.

Scene Seventeen

Next day. Marcelo with the shoeshine kit. A customer comes along and he starts shoeshining. Mariza comes on stealthily behind him. She grabs the kit. The Man loses his balance. Marcelo is quick to get hold of the kit. Mariza and Marcelo pull at the kit and shout at each other.

Marcelo and Mariza It's mine! Let it go! Leave it!

Man Blasted urchins! Scamps!

The kit falls. Mariza and Marcelo grapple over it. The angry Man starts to hit them. Rambo comes on. He's got a knife. He goes for the Man. The Man runs off.

Rambo Stop, you two!

Mariza and Marcelo stop. Rambo speaks to Mariza.

Now. You've failed, Mariza.

Mariza I got my kit back.

Marcelo I caught her!

Rambo	Marcelo caught you. You shouldn't have let him catch you.
	Mariza gets up and starts to leave.
Anita	She fought for it.
	Mariza stops.
Mariza	I fought for it!
Anita	She can fight.
	Rambo assessing the damage to Marcelo.
Marcelo	She bit my nose.
Rambo	Has she? Okay, you can stay in the gang.
	Mariza suddenly lights up with happiness.
	Get back to work.
	Mariza rushes to pick up the bits of the kit. They exit.

Scene Eighteen

A favela. Anita enters and gestures off to Mariza to come forward.

Anita	Come on.
Mariza	Are you sure your mum will like me?
Anita	Don't worry, my mum is really lovely. She loves my friends. She's a very good mum.
Mariza	Is she beautiful?
Anita	My mum's very beautiful. You see what a nice shack we have? It's tin not cardboard.
	They enter the shack.
	Mum?
	Anita's Dad speaks from offstage.
Dad	Who is it?
	He enters.
	Anita?

Anita	Hello, Dad. This is my friend Mariza.
Dad	Hello, Mariza.
Mariza	Hello.

Mariza keeps her eyes on Anita's Dad.

Anita	How are things, Dad?
Dad	As usual. Getting worse.

Mariza is spellbound and whispers to Anita.

Mariza	Have you got a dad?
Dad	I lost my job down the market. So I stick to doing little jobs, repairing the shack. Have you been all right?
Anita	Yes, Dad.

Mariza whispers again.

Mariza	A real dad?

Anita whispers to Mariza.

Anita	Yes.

She speaks to her Dad.

I'm getting tired of living on the street.

Dad	Anita, you can always stay here.
Anita	And Mum?
Dad	Your mum should be here any minute. What about your friend Mariza?
Anita	Her mum lost her.
Mariza	I lost my mum on the road one night.
Dad	And you've never seen her since?
Mariza	No. I never had a dad.

There is a pause.

Dad	Will you stay at home, Anita?
Anita	Only if I don't get hassled.
Dad	Well, you know how it is. I really didn't expect you to run away like your brother.

Act One, Scene Eighteen

Anita speaks to Mariza.

Anita My brother has had enough and run away.

Dad Boys don't think twice about running away. They're not like girls. They just go. Your poor mother, who loved your brother so much. And you. You know how much Mum loves you, don't you?

Anita holds out two tins.

Anita I've found some beans.

Dad Oh, from the rubbish, eh?

Anita Yes!

Dad They don't look too rusty at all. Will you eat with us, Mariza?

Mariza Can I call you Dad?

Dad What?

Anita whispers.

Anita Mariza never had a dad.

Mariza Can I call you Dad?

Dad Of course, Mariza. Do call me Dad. There's no harm in that.

Mariza smiles. Seeing this, so do Anita and her Dad.

Now, let me put these beans in the saucepan.

Mum comes in. She is in a great hurry.

Mum Who's there?

Anita doesn't answer.

Oh, it's you.

Anita Yes, Mum.

Mum Have you come back, have you?

Anita doesn't answer.

I expect you to behave this time, Anita. Otherwise you're out. Anything to eat, Daddy.

Dad is obviously intimidated.

Dad Er . . . Ehm . . .

Anita whispers.

Anita   Beans.

Dad   Oh, beans!

Mum   Beans, eh? Good! And you told me you had no money for food!

Dad   Anita brought a couple of tins.

Mum   Ah, good. What a lovely daughter we have.

Anita   Mum, this is Mariza.

Mum   What's she doing here?

Anita   She's with me.

Mariza   Can I call you Mum?

Mum   Eh? Where're these beans, man!

Dad   They won't take a minute.

Mum   I'm starving. This is a blasted life this is! Your brother left! I have to work as a cleaner in a skyscraper! Your father without a job. What life is this, eh? Lucky there's this.

She drinks from a bottle in her bag.

Dad   Stop drinking.

Mum drinks again.

Leave that!

Mum   Don't think I don't know you drink all my leftovers! That's all your dad's good at!

Dad tries to get the bottle off her. She pushes him away. Dad falls down.

Mariza   Dad!

Mariza and Anita help Dad up.

Are you all right, Dad?

Mum   What did you say?

Mariza doesn't answer.

What did you say?

Mariza doesn't answer.

She called you Dad! You never told me you had another child.

Dad She's not my child!

Mum Liar! I heard her call you Dad!

Anita whispers to Mariza.

Anita He's not your dad.

Mum You had another child from another woman and you never told me! You good for nothing! And you children! The scum of the earth! You're worthless!

Dad pushes off the drunk Mum. Mum brandishes the bottle. Dad and the two girls run off.

You had another child and you never told me!

Scene Nineteen

Anita and Mariza run on, breathless.

Anita You see what you have done?

Mariza What?

Anita You made my mum angry.

Mariza is confused. Dad joins them. He is out of breath.

Mariza Dad?

Dad I'm not your dad!

Anita He's not your dad!

Mariza is hurt.

Dad Anita, your mum was so drunk she thought Mariza was my daughter with another wife. Tomorrow, your mum'll be sober. I'll explain to her that Mariza is your friend and not my daughter. Only tonight, we cannot go back home.

Mariza We can go and sleep in the rubbish pit.

Dad	Rubbish pit? You sleep in the rubbish pit?
Anita	Nobody bothers you there. The cops don't come there.
Dad	What about the smell? No, I'll stay here. Awake just in case your mum –

Anita speaks to Mariza.

Anita	We can sleep here too.

Mariza replies promptly, again wanting to be part of the family.

Mariza	Yes.

They settle down to sleep.

Dad?

Dad	Why don't you sleep?
Mariza	You won't go away, will you?
Dad	No, I won't go anywhere.

Dad cries.

Mariza	Why are you crying, Dad?
Anita	Shhh.
Dad	Why have children if one has to suffer from it! I wish I never was a father! You can't look after them. You can't give them an education or a future. Nothing.

There is a pause. Dad checks Mariza and Anita are asleep and leaves. Mariza wakes up.

Mariza	Dad? Dad?
Anita	Shut up!
Mariza	He's left us! I knew he would! I was spying on him! Dad!
Anita	He's not your dad! He's not your dad! He's my dad!
Mariza	He said.
Anita	My dad only said to call him Dad!
Mariza	He didn't mean it?
Anita	No. My dad was just being kind. Okay?

Act One, Scene Nineteen

There is a pause.

Mariza And your mum?

Anita My mum's my mum. She's not your mum. If she was your mum we would be sisters! But we are not sisters! So, she's only my mum, not yours.

Another pause.

Mariza My mum is not like your mum anyway. My mum's nicer.

Anita My mum is very nice! All right! It was the wrong day. Any other day, my mum's really wonderful. The best in the world.

An angry Rambo comes on. He has the shoeshine kit.

Rambo Where have you been?

Mariza We went to see –

Anita I went to see my mum. Mariza came along.

Rambo pushes her.

Rambo I'm responsible for you! You tell me where you go! Every time! What about work, eh?

Anita It was a long time I hadn't seen mum.

Rambo Come on, start working.

Mariza Don't you have a mum, Rambo?

Rambo No mummy talk, okay?

Mariza replies tentatively.

Mariza Why?

Rambo snaps back, making the others jump.

Rambo I don't want to hear about mums!

He calms down.

I hated my mum. I just couldn't stand her. When my father left her she got another husband, he really was nasty with me, beating me black and blue every day. So I went to stay with my father and stepmother. My stepmum, she was wonderful. I liked my stepmum more than my own mum. My stepmum was really nice, but she had too many children of her own to look after. Come on, get working.

Mariza prepares the shoeshine kit.

Look, you only need a mum when you're a baby, because you can't walk. But once you've started to walk on your own two feet, who needs a mum, eh? Not me, the street is my mama. It gives me everything I want, food, friends, enemies.

The sinister figure stalks the street. It comes towards them. Rambo flashes out his knife.

Go away!

But the figure moves forward.

I'll cut you! I'll make mincemeat of you!

The figure stops and withdraws. Anita shivers with fear.

Anita Blimey. Gives me the creeps.

Mariza Who was that? One of the killers?

Rambo It's not your business. I don't want you to have anything to do with such scum. Okay?

The girls nod, scared by the figure. They follow Rambo out. The figure stalks after them.

Scene Twenty

Mum comes on, still carrying Mariza's coat. She approaches a passerby.

Mum Excuse me, Senhor? I'm looking for my daughters.

Man Your daughters?

Mum I lost them. One night. Have you perhaps seen a couple of girls, one twelve, the other eight.

Man Don't you know how many streetkids there are in this town? Thousands of them.

Act One, Scene Twenty

Mum What else a mother can do? The police won't help me.

Man No, they wouldn't. Lost daughters, eh? Like looking for a needle in a haystack.

A gunshot offstage catches their attention. Tania staggers on. She is in a much worse state than last time we saw her. Having been living on the streets for months.

Mum Tania?

Tania turns towards her mother.

Tania Mum?

Mum Tania. Thank God, I've found you.

Tania I'm wounded, Mum.

Mum Wounded?

She shows the stolen loaf.

And Mariza? What's happened to Mariza?

Tania I left her on the road that night. A bad man gave me money and took me away. When I went back Mariza wasn't there anymore. Only the rope. Mum.

She dies. A Cop comes on with the gun still in his hand. He puts it away. He looks at the body, picks up the loaf and exits.

Man One of your lost children?

Mum Oh, Tania! Now I've lost you again. Forever. I looked so hard for you. If I knew I'd find you dead I would have not moved from the spot on the road where I left you. What wrong have you done to be killed like this? For stealing bread!

Man It happens every day.

Mum Every day? It's become normal to kill children, has it?

Man You should have taught your daughter not to steal.

Mum How could I teach her to go hungry?

Man You didn't teach her to refuse money from strangers.

Mum How could I teach that to my Tania? Who else was there to provide her with food and clothes?

Man A mum should love her child enough to protect her.

Mum I loved her! What other mother would have gone begging and living on the street to find her children? But a mum's love is not enough when nobody helps you. She was innocent and young. After so many sacrifices to bring them up in this cruel world. Tania! What's happened to your little sister? Is my Mariza still alive? How can I go on now, looking for Mariza. This is how I'll find Mariza as well.

Man If you didn't know how to provide for your children, you shouldn't have brought them into the world.

Mum Yes. You're right. I'll forget I had two daughters. I'll tell myself I'm not, I never was, a mother. I never gave birth to living things. I never had a family.

Scene Twenty-one

Mariza comes on with her shoeshine kit. At her back the sinister Figure appears and approaches slowly. When it gets close behind Mariza, the Figure lifts up the rolled-up carpet-like thing it is carrying. It looks as though it is going to strike Mariza. Mariza senses someone behind her and turns.

Mariza Aaaaaaahhhh!

She freezes in terror. Suddenly the rolled up thing in the Figure's hand rolls open. It is a gigantic multiplication table. The Figure speaks threateningly.

Figure One by one, one. Two by two, four –

Suddenly the Figure's intonation changes into a teacher-like intonation, welcoming participation from Mariza.

Four by four, sixteen.
Five by five, twenty-five.

Six by six, thirty-six.
Let's start again.
One by one? One.
Mariza is trembling.

Mariza One.
Like an enchanter, the Figure withdraws with the table and with Mariza following.

Figure Two by two? Four.
Mariza Four.
Figure Three by three? Nine.
Mariza Nine.

End of Act One.

ACT TWO

Scene One

Mariza, Anita, Marcelo and other streetkids assembled around the street Teacher who is giving them a pavement class lesson. The Teacher is dressed like the Figure in Act One. She is a blind woman and indicates the numbers on the table with unfailing strokes of her cane. They all chorus together.

Teacher One by one, one! Two by two, four!

As this continues Rambo comes on. Seeing him and knowing of his disapproval, the kids scatter away. The Teacher senses Rambo. To avoid a violent confrontation, slowly and calmly she rolls up her table.

Rambo I won't have any of my gang learning anything! We've all run away and skived school. We're not going back to that! In the street you don't need to read and write! You only need to be sharp and tough! I won't have you skiving work for school!

The Teacher speaks tentatively.

Teacher Rambo –

Rambo Now, what does the missionary want here, eh?

Teacher Reading and writing are very important.

Rambo What about food and clothes?

Teacher You don't like school because it doesn't give you free books and pencils. And your parents can't afford them.

Rambo The teacher we had couldn't even find Brazil on the map! Ha! Ha! Ha!

Rambo gives the kids a hard look and they automatically laugh with him.

Teacher It's very important for you to learn how to count and use numbers. If you don't, other people will take advantage of you.

Rambo runs and holds on to the Teacher.

Rambo Anybody who takes advantage of me, right, they won't be alive to enjoy it.

Teacher Let go of me.

Rambo What have you got on you?

Teacher Nothing.

Rambo You want to help? Give us money, come on!

Teacher I haven't got any money.

Rambo gestures to Anita who quickly goes through the Teacher's pockets. There isn't any money.

I don't carry money with me.

Rambo 'I don't carry money with me'.

Rambo lets go of the Teacher.

We only need teachers who carry money, okay? We need to eat every day, remember.

Teacher The organisation I work for is going to open a Drop-in Centre for Streetkids. You'll be able to get a free lunch there.

Rambo When?

Teacher In a month, or two.

Rambo What do we eat now, eh?

Teacher Now?

Rambo Yes! Now! We're hungry now! Now! What do you want for lunch, gang? Food or maths!

The gang members have various replies.

Gang Food! Lunch! Sandwiches!

Rambo You see?

Teacher Yes, I know.

Rambo You see, your lessons are all right for kids who have their parents who give them lunch and dinners. If my gang here listens to your lessons, how the hell are they going to find something to eat?

Teacher Yes, I do understand.
Rambo You do understand? What?
Teacher You must eat first.
Rambo Right. You're learning fast, Teacher. Good.

Rambo turns to the gang.

Now let us get on with finding food, okay?

Rambo pushes the Teacher off.

Get lost or we'll eat you. Hang on, I like your coat. Give it here.

Teacher No.

Rambo takes the coat and puts it on.

Rambo Now move!

He pushes the Teacher off. He struts with the new coat on to the admiring eyes of the gang.

Well, I gave the teacher a lesson. It's only right I get paid for it.

He exits followed by the others.

Scene Two

A street. Traffic noise. Mariza comes on with her shoeshine kit. She also has her battered doll with an arm and a leg missing. At the same time, Anita comes on and begs on the opposite pavement. A scrunched paper bag is discarded from a passing vehicle into the middle of the road. Mariza is going for it but then, seeing Anita anticipating her, remains on the edge of the pavement. Mariza warns Anita of the oncoming vehicle.

Mariza Anita!

Anita makes it back just in time as the vehicle speeds past her. She dashes for the paper bag and, zig-

Act Two, Scene Two

zagging dangerously amongst the traffic, gets to Mariza's side of the road.

What's in it?

Anita Bits of sandwich.

Anita stuffs it in her mouth.

Mariza Give me some!

Anita swallows.

Anita It's gone! I wish I had a doll. Every girl has got one. Nobody ever bought me a doll.

Mariza This was my sister's, Tania's.

Anita Dolls are very good. They never hassle you.

Mariza A mum tells a child what to do. If you have a doll then you'll be her mum.

Anita snatches the doll from Mariza. Mariza is going for it.

Anita I only want to hold her. Mariza, when I have a doll, I'll clean her and take her to school. I'd dress her nicely first. I wouldn't let her be a streetkid.

Mariza takes the doll back.

Mariza Anita, I want you to see my mum.

Anita Have you found her?

Mariza Over there.

They move to a poster with a picture of Linda Carter as 'Wonderwoman' on it. A passerby is listening keenly to a radio, reacting to the football game being transmitted. It looks as though the man is having a discussion verging on argument with the radio.

Anita What's this?

Mariza She's my mum.

Mariza notices the man listening to the radio.

Anita Is your mum famous? Is she a singer?

Mariza Ehm. Sometimes. Look how wonderful she is, and smiling.

Anita   This is her name.

Mariza   What does it say?

Anita puts a finger on each letter, trying to read but without success.

Anita   Maybe the teacher knows how to read it. What's your mum's name?

Mariza   Ehm.

She makes it up, following the letters like Anita and pretending to read them.

E-s-t-r-e-lla! Estrella.

Anita   Es-trel-la. How do we find her?

Mariza   She sings on the radio.

Anita   Maybe we can speak to a radio.

Mariza   You can't speak to a radio.

Anita   Yes, you can. Like a telephone. You turn the knob this way and that and you can hear all sorts of people speaking and singing. When you hear your mum, you talk to her.

Mariza nods, impressed by Anita's knowledge. Anita approaches the man and indicates to him the shoeshine kit. He thinks a bit and then decides he will have his shoes cleaned. The radio station is transmitting a football game in English. Mariza and Anita listen for a bit. Mariza whispers to Anita.

Mariza   I don't understand. What language is that?

Anita   Shhh.

Unseen by the Man, Anita turns the station knob. It speaks Brazilian Portuguese. The Man, a bit surprised, re-adjusts it. Anita does it again.

Man   What the hell's going on here!

He re-adjusts it again. The girls continue shoeshining. The Man suddenly shouts.

Goal!

Act Two, Scene Two

Mariza and Anita start back.

We are winning! We're winning! One–nil!

Anita Excuse me, Senhor.

The Man is pre-occupied with the radio.

Man Uh?

Anita Can you please tell her mum she is here.

Man What?

Anita Her mum . . . sings on the radio.

The Man's attention is on the radio.

Man Oh, yes.

He speaks to the radio.

Ernesto! Shoot!

Anita Can you please tell her mum. Her name's Estrella. She's a singer. Can you ask her to speak to her daughter?

The Man's attention is still on the game.

Man Who's the daughter of a singer?

Anita Her.

Mariza Me.

Anita points to the poster.

Anita That's her mum.

Man A singer? That's an actress.

Anita speaks to Mariza.

Anita An actress?

Mariza She is on the radio.

Man Is she?

Mariza Sometimes.

Man Well, I'm not surprised. She's a famous American actress! Superwoman. You are her daughter?

Mariza replies sincerely.

Mariza Yes.

The Man looks at Mariza's scruffy appearance.

Man No kidding?

Anita asks Mariza suspiciously.

Anita Are you really sure she is . . .?

Mariza cuts in.

Mariza My mum's very rich . . . and beautiful.

Man And she left you on the street? With all her money?

Mariza She left me on the road one night.

The Man addresses the poster.

Man What a horror!

Mariza Why are you calling my mum that?

Man Why!? She shouldn't have left her daughter on the streets, that's why.

Suddenly he shouts.

Goal!

But it is the opposite team.

Oh! No! They've equalised. Your mum, eh? A bad mother.

Suddenly to the radio.

Pass the ball, Ernesto! Come on, Ricardo! No! What have you done! Not a penalty!? You son of a gun! I hate you, ref!

Mariza Can you please make my mum speak on the radio?

Man What you mean?

Anita If you change the station.

Man Hey! Hey! Hey! What are you talking about? There's the final on, are you crazy, nothing in the world will make me miss the final. Have you finished with it?

Mariza nods 'No' and continues shoeshining. Anita is looking closely at the poster. Rambo comes on casually behind the Man. Rambo makes a sign to Mariza and Anita not to take notice of him. The Man suddenly shouts.

Goal! We have! No they have. We, they –

Suddenly, Rambo snatches the radio, shoves the Man down and runs off.

Ah! My radio! The final! You scamp! The final! Who scored! Who scored! Are we winning? Are we losing?

Anita Senhor, the money.

Man You're the scum of the earth! You streetkids! Hooligans! You should be in reform school! Where they beat you all the time!

He runs off in Rambo's direction.

My radio! My radio! Police! Police!

Rambo comes on from another direction. He uses the radio to dance to.

Anita When I grow up I'd like to be like Rambo. Isn't he nice?

Mariza Yes.

Anita He's my boyfriend.

Mariza He's 'my' boyfriend.

Anita I'll marry Rambo.

Mariza He'll marry me first.

Anita Rambo promised me.

They fight, screaming Aaaaahhhh! Aaaaaaahhh! Rambo exits dancing to the radio.

Scene Three

A football pitch in the favela. Streetkids playing football with an imaginary ball. They play with a fierce passion. Mariza stops playing and is trying to talk to Anita in the opposite team. At last, Mariza manages to stop Anita.

Anita Let go of me!

Mariza insists Anita go with her.

I want to play football.

Mariza insists.

I don't want to know!

Mariza insists.

I don't want to know! We play football on a Sunday! It's bad luck to go working on a Sunday!

Marcelo is frustrated by the interruption.

Marcelo What are you doing?

Rambo Eh! You two!

Marcelo Are you playing or what?!

Rambo Hang on.

Anita Mariza wants me to go to town. To look for her mum!

Marcelo You keep stopping the game!

Mariza insists.

Anita I don't want to know about your mum!

Rambo Get out of the way.

Marcelo Just get out of the pitch.

They push Mariza off the pitch and the playing resumes. After a while Mariza is back with a football. She is staring at it with unbelieving eyes.

Get out!

Anita Get lost!

But Mariza advances onto the pitch. The others are going to push her off the pitch again, but they remain stunned by the sight of the football. Slowly recovering, they gesture Mariza to let them have the ball.

Mariza I found it! It's mine!

Apart from Rambo, the others close in on and attack Mariza, each wanting to get the ball for themselves. Rambo gestures he wants the ball. Whoever's got it gives it to him. The others look on, not daring to challenge Rambo. Mariza is crying.

It's mine! I found it! It's mine!

Act Two, Scene Three

A push from Rambo sends Mariza reeling back. She comes forward again, but Rambo's further threats make her back away. Rambo places the ball delicately on the ground to start the match.

Rambo Listen, gang! Don't you dare kick it too hard. Anyone who hurts 'my' ball is dead. All right?

Anita How can we play if we don't kick the ball?

Marcelo How can we play if –

Rambo cuts in.

Rambo All right!

General noises of protest from the others. Rambo threatens to take the ball away with him. A chorus of agreement from the others stop him. At last the match resumes. Anita kicks the ball. Rambo slaps her.

I am first!

Rambo goes to kick the ball but misses it. He tries again. This time he hits the ground in front of the ball. Muffled giggles from the others. He tries again clumsily dribbling, with nobody else moving, Rambo gets to the goal but realises he has left the ball behind. He tries to hide his humiliation.

Okay. You can all kick 'my' ball. Only make sure you kick it properly.

Anita Not like you then?

Rambo gives Anita a deadly look and then advances on her. Anita backs away scared. Rambo gestures a threat to her and returns to the ball.

Just let's get on with it!

Rambo Shut up! Mind it doesn't go down the hill! Into the sewers! The other gang'll nick it!

Mariza I've found it! It's 'my' ball!

Rambo I'll slap you! Right, let's start.

He speaks to Mariza.

Hey, you want to play?

Mariza Yes!

The teams reform. The game resumes but they all have trouble playing with a 'real' ball. They keep missing it, hitting the ground, hitting each other's legs, etc. They pause, utterly bewildered by this.

Anita The police!

All The police! The police!

Siren noise. They scatter away and hide. A Cop comes on. Rambo goes back for the ball but the Cop is standing by it. As he goes for the ball the Cop grabs him.

Cop Where's the radio? The radio you mugged yesterday, where is it?

Rambo You want it for yourself, don't you.

Cop Just give me the radio.

Rambo No way.

Cop I'll kill you if you don't.

Rambo I don't know anything about the radio.

The Cop takes the ball and pushes Rambo off with him. The others come out slowly from their hiding places.

Anita What we do now?

Marcelo Let's go to the shopping centre.

Mariza Yes, I'm hungry.

Anita Starving.

Marcelo I'd eat anything.

Mariza It was my ball.

They exit.

Scene Four

Mum enters with a bundle made up of Mariza's coat and a piece of wood in it.

Mum My child, my child, my child. I'll never leave you. I'll

Act Two, Scene Four

never leave you. You'll always be with me. I'll never leave you. Never, never, never.

The Cop comes on, sees Mum and approaches her.

Cop You know the score, don't you?

Mum You killed my daughter.

Cop She was a thief.

Mum You killed my Tania for a loaf of bread.

The Cop looks into Mum's bundle.

Cop It's a bundle.

Mum It's my Mariza.

Cop It's a fake bundle.

Mum No.

Cop Yes, it is! Throw it away, will you.

Mum I wouldn't have a real child anymore. I want a child who can never die, a child I can never have to abandon. A child who doesn't need anything.

The Cop takes the bundle from her. He takes out the piece of wood.

Cop A piece of wood. I like that.

Mum My Mariza.

Cop Now let me tell you the score.

Mum Is my Mariza still alive?

Cop If you want to beg in this area, fifty per cent of what you make goes to me. You understand?

Mum I never abandoned her.

Cop Mad woman, I'm talking to you!

He pushes the bundle into Mum's arms.

Fifty per cent of what you beg is for me.

Mum Mariza'll never never understand. I never abandoned her!

Cop If you don't pay up, you won't be allowed to beg here. You understand, mad woman?

Mum I'm tired ... tired. Always looking for my Mariza. I'm much happier to have a piece of wood for a daughter than a real child.

The Cop exits.

They won't steal or hurt this one. They won't kill this one. You murderers! You won't kill this one.

Scene Five

The Baker comes on with his bakery. He is tying up a large cake box with a ribbon. Mariza comes on, peeps in and then waits in front of the Baker's. The Baker comes out.

Baker Hey! You're one of Rambo's mob, aren't you?

Mariza Yes.

Baker Well, where's Rambo then?

Mariza shrugs.

Jesus! If the scamp is not here in the next minute, he'll never work for me again! I told him to be here at three!

Marcelo runs by.

Mariza Marcelo!

Marcelo Mariza. They've killed Rambo.

The Baker overhears.

Baker What!?

Marcelo speaks to Mariza.

Marcelo Rambo. I've seen his body under the bridge . . . I'm off to tell the others.

Marcelo runs off.

Baker Jesus! You really can't trust these streetkids! To get killed on me like that! The moment I need him most! The cake! Who is going to deliver it now! Who?

Mariza starts to leave.

Hey! Come here! You used to go with Rambo to deliver my bread, didn't you?

Mariza Yes.

Baker You know the Parco Real then?

Mariza nods.

And the big house? The pink one? On the right of the Park, with railings and grounds and tall trees?

Mariza nods. The Baker wonders whether to trust her.

What choice have I got! A birthday cake it's no good tomorrow, is it? Do you want to do it for me?

Mariza Ehm.

Baker You'll get the same as Rambo. Forty cruzados.

Mariza is amazed.

Mariza Forty?

Baker Yes, it's a rich house. Here.

He gives Mariza the box, plus a pen and a receipt.

Bring the receipt back to me.

Mariza starts to go, then hesitates, almost wanting to give the box back.

Hey! You told me you know the way! Do you or don't you?

Mariza Yes.

Baker Come on! Shake a leg! The cake's for this birthday not the next one!

Mariza exits.

Scene Six

The grounds of a mansion. Two kids from the house come on and start playing picnic with a doll. Anita comes on and stands at the railings, looking at them. The kids' talk is indistinct. The two kids eat sandwiches and casually throw bits at Anita who catches them or picks them up and eats them. Mariza comes on and goes by carrying the cake box. Recognising Anita, she tries not to attract her attention. But as soon as she has passed, Anita whispers.

Anita Mariza.
Mariza doesn't stop. Anita whispers again.
Mariza.
Mariza doesn't stop. Anita whispers louder.
Mariza!!
Mariza whispers.

Mariza What you want?

Anita What's that?

Mariza Anita –

Anita A cake, ain't it?

Mariza I don't know.

Anita I'm starving.

Mariza I have to deliver it!

Anita Any . . . any chance to . . . I mean –

Mariza You crazy!?

Anita Come on.

Mariza Get off!

Anita It's so big! Nobody'll notice a bite!

Mariza I'll get forty cruzados for it!

Anita Forty? I'll come with you.

Mariza Yesterday, right? The orange juice. You didn't give any, did you?

Anita With forty cruzados we can buy a hamburger. Chips as well.
Mariza scowls negatively and starts to go. Anita pulls her back.
See them?

Mariza I ain't interested.

Anita Playing with a doll?

Mariza pauses.

Mariza A doll?

Anita Yeah. Looks like the doll I always wanted.

Mariza starts to go but, unable to resist, joins Anita in staring at the two kids in the grounds. The two kids don't pay any attention to them. Mariza realises she must deliver the cake. She enters the gate with Anita.

Kid 1 I wish they'd go away.

Kid 2 They're ever so dirty.

Kid 1 They stink.

Kid 2 Do you know they live in the sewers?

Kid 1 Not these two?

Kid 2 Yes! They do!

Kid 1 Uh, I think you're right.

Kid 2 Why don't they go back to the streets?

Kid 1 They've come to deliver something.

Kid 2 I wish they'd go away.

Kid 1 Astor? Where's Astor?

The two kids stare hard at Mariza and Anita. Then they go off looking for Astor, their dog. Mariza starts to go towards the front door. Anita has stopped and started to play with the doll. Mariza stops and whispers.

Mariza Don't do that!

But Anita continues. Mariza gets back to her.

We must deliver the cake!

Anita Now you play.

Mariza hesitates.

Mariza Only for a minute.

Mariza plays with the doll. She gets very engrossed in it. Unseen by her, Anita opens the box and, famished, starts to eat the cake. Suddenly Astor, the watchdog, comes growling towards Mariza. Anita runs away.

Anita Mariza! Take the doll with you!

Suddenly the kids have appeared and they all bark ferociously in unison. Mariza screams, drops the doll and runs off after Anita.

Kid 1 Get them, Astor!
Kid 2 Kill them!
Kid 1 Thieves!
Kid 2 Have they stolen anything?
Kid 1 Astor stopped them.
Kid 2 Well done, Astor.

They gather their picnic things together.

Kid 1 Come on, Astor. Let's go.
Kid 2 You deserve a bit of dad's birthday cake, Astor.

Kid 1 is horrified.

Kid 1 Dad's birthday cake!
Kid 2 They've eaten it all up!
Kid 1 Urchins!
Kid 2 Dad'll go mad!

They exit.

Scene Seven

Anita and Mariza come on. Suddenly . . .

Mariza Ah!
Anita It's only a rat.
Mariza It sounded really big.
Anita It can only be a rat.
Mariza Like that dog.
Anita Forget the dog.

Act Two, Scene Seven

They sit down.

At last. I think it's safe here. Have you got any money for a sandwich, Mariza?

Mariza We lost the Baker's money! Because you started playing with the doll.

Anita You shouldn't have dropped the doll.

Mariza I don't care about the doll!

Mariza Hey! What's the matter with you! I really wanted that doll, all right!

Mariza I wanted to deliver the cake and get the Baker's money!

Anita I saved you from the dog!

Mariza You ate the cake while I was playing.

There is a pause. Marcelo comes on, carrying a bundle. He deposits it in front of them. They open it. In it there are Rambo's clothes and the football. They look at them for a moment.

Marcelo I'll keep the ball.

Anita Why should you have it?

Mariza Why?

Marcelo Why should you have it then?

Anita I want the belt!

Marcelo All right. Only for today, all right?

Anita We'll see about that. Mariza should have the football.

Mariza I don't want it.

Anita You found it, Mariza.

Marcelo What about me? These trousers won't fit me.

Anita You already got Rambo's trainers on!

Marcelo I got them on to play football.

Anita The ball's Mariza's!

Marcelo I saw Rambo dead first.

Anita gets up to fight Marcelo. Mariza screams.

Mariza I don't want it! I don't want no bleeding football!

The others stop and wait for Mariza to calm down.

I want the cap. Rambo's cap. He took it from me when you found me in the rubbish.

Anita looks into the bundle.

Anita It's not here.

Marcelo No.

Anita They didn't give Rambo's cap?

Marcelo They said it was too dirty . . . with blood.

There is a pause. Each takes bits of what there is.

Scene Eight

A street. Christmas sounds everywhere. It is raining softly or snowing and very cold. There is not much traffic. Anita starts begging. Mariza comes on, on the other pavement, selling bracelets. Kids go by with boxes of presents, paying no attention to Mariza or Anita. Then an isolated car goes by. From its window a large box with a picture of a doll on it is thrown out. Anita sees it and dashes to pick up the box. The sound of a braking truck very close by is heard and Mariza realises what is happening. She sees the truck, running over Anita. She runs towards the body, passersby stop. From their comments and gestures, it is clear that Anita is dead. Some people, or ambulancemen, take away Anita's body. The doll's box has dropped back to the ground still unopened. Mariza takes it and goes back to the pavement. She continues to sell bracelets, but without conviction. The Teacher comes on, with her table. She is looking for streetkids willing to hear her lessons.

Teacher Hello.

There is a pause.

Are you on your own?

Act Two, Scene Eight   **127**

                Another pause.
                Where's your friend . . . Anita?
                Another pause.
                Do you remember me? The teacher?
                Mariza looks up.
                Are you all right?
                Another pause.
                What's the matter with you? You look very sad.

Mariza   I have not eaten anything.

Teacher   Nothing all day?

Mariza   Nobody has given me anything. Nobody. They kill you if you steal to eat.

Teacher   It's my lunch. But you can have it.

                She gives her a sandwich. Mariza takes it then gives it back.
                Aren't you hungry?
                Mariza nods.
                Well, eat then.

Mariza   It's yours.

Teacher   I'm giving it to you.

                Mariza shakes her head.
                You'll die if you don't eat anything.

Mariza   I want to die.

Teacher   Have it. Go on.

Mariza   All my friends are dead. Rambo.

Teacher   Yes, I heard about Rambo.

Mariza   Anita.

Teacher   Anita? When?

Mariza   Just now. Run over. A box with a doll in it. This one . . . they threw it out of a car into the road. Anita . . . she dashes to get the doll. But a car comes and runs her over. Anita always wanted a doll. I haven't opened it yet.

The Teacher takes the box and opens it.

Teacher There's nothing in it.

Mariza It's empty? Anita thought . . . she believed there was a doll in it. The doll she always wanted.

Mariza is calm, almost indifferent.

Now I'll die as well.

Teacher Aren't you scared to die?

Mariza No. All streetkids die.

Teacher If you die you'll never find your mum. Have you forgotten about your mum?

Mariza No.

Teacher She might be looking for you.

Mariza I don't think so. She lives in America now.

Teacher How do you know?

Mariza She is a singer. She's too busy to look for me. She's always flying in planes from one city to the other.

Teacher Do you want to come with me?

Mariza No.

Teacher The charity I work for has opened a Drop-in Centre for kids like you.

Mariza No.

Teacher You'll eat . . . you'll have a shower. You cannot stay the night. But if you come every day I'll teach you to read and write.

Mariza Rambo said we don't need to learn anything.

Teacher Everybody needs to learn.

Mariza I will soon die, like all the other streetkids.

There is a pause.

Teacher I was once a streetkid like you.

Mariza I don't believe you.

Teacher And when I was a streetkid, you know what I used to do?

Act Two, Scene Eight

The Teacher goes into a busking act she used to do. For a moment, Mariza seems interested, but then she plunges back into her sad indifference.

And people gave me some coins. But I couldn't go on for ever. Especially after Rambo blinded me.

Mariza Rambo blinded you?

Teacher Yes, I was in another gang. And one night there was a big fight around this bonfire we used to have. And Rambo takes a burning stick from the bonfire and hits me, across the face, over the eyes. I lost my sight. But then I was very lucky because a street teacher helped me. He taught me to read and write. Now I want to help other people.

Mariza Everybody spits at me and calls me thief. If I ask for food they say I've got scabies and chase me away. It's better to die.

Teacher You see, Mariza, the first thing you must learn is that your life is very important. No one in the world, whoever they are, no one is more important than you and your life. You must not end up like Anita or Rambo.

There is a pause.

Mariza Do you have a mum?

Teacher Ehm . . . No. I had a granny, that's all. But she was too old to teach me anything or look after me. Tomorrow, come to the Drop-in Centre.

Mariza No.

Mariza starts to leave.

Teacher Think about it.

Mariza I just want to die.

Teacher I tell you what, if you come to the Centre I'll let you call me Mum!

Mariza stops.

Mariza Mum?

Teacher Yes.

The Teacher exits.

Scene Nine

Mum comes on with the bundle. She has a plastic flower. She talks to the bundle.

Mum People think me mad for having a child of wood. Little girls have dolls, little boys teddy bears, why shouldn't I have you? My little wooden baby. A year ago I was selling flowers with Tania and Mariza. Since I lost my two girls everything's got worse. Life it's so hard. It's not worth living anymore. Two flowers. I begged all day to buy them. We left one on Tania's little grave, didn't we? And this other one? Yes, it's for my Mariza. She must be dead too. What chance would a little girl have in a cruel world like this? But we don't even know where Mariza's been buried, do we? Here. You have the flower, my little wooden baby.

Scene Ten

The Drop-in Centre. The Teacher comes on with a chair. Suddenly, an anxious Marcelo runs in as if someone is pursuing him.

Teacher Who's it?

Marcelo Marcelo.

Teacher Oh, yes, Marcelo. It's two months after your last lesson. Let's see if you remember anything.
Marcelo gestures a desperate 'Spare me, please!'
Five by five?
Marcelo pays no attention.

Marcelo Ehm . . . twelve.

Act Two, Scene Ten

Teacher Twenty-five. Two by two?
Marcelo Two by two? Oh, four!
Teacher Good. Well done. Smashing, Marcelo.
Marcelo It was nothing.
Teacher Something a bit more difficult then. Three by three?
Marcelo Ehm . . . twelve.

The Teacher rebukes Marcelo.

Teacher Marcelo.
Marcelo Please, Auntie, give me something to eat.
Teacher You only come here when you're in trouble.
Marcelo No, honest, I'm here to learn. Three by three is . . . is . . . If I put three plus three plus three it makes, makes . . . plus plus plus.

He goes to check the door.

Teacher Who's after you?
Marcelo How can I worry about five by five and six by six!
Teacher The police?
Marcelo They want to kill me.
Teacher I warned you last time.
Marcelo I got in with some old friends. They stole. So I had to steal with them.

The Teacher feels and smells his clothes.

Teacher How dirty you are.
Marcelo Auntie, another streetkid told me one can have a shower and new clothes here.
Teacher Only if you promise you won't go back stealing again.
Marcelo I promise. Hang on! What will I eat if I don't steal? Nobody employs me. They say at nine I'm too young for work! But I have to eat! And clothe myself! And I need trainers! How do I get these things if nobody gives me work? I've got no parents who buy things for me, have I?
Teacher Well, just be careful not to get in too much trouble.

Marcelo	Cross my heart, Auntie.
Teacher	I'm not your auntie, Marcelo.
Marcelo	Yes, Auntie. I mean Senhorita. Anything you say.
Teacher	I've only got a spare T-shirt. Here.
	Marcelo puts on the clean T-shirt. Mariza comes in. It is her first time there.
	Hello?
	Marcelo whispers.
Marcelo	It's Mariza.
Teacher	Hello, Mariza.
	The Teacher offers her hand to shake. Very quickly Mariza takes the watch from her wrist.
	What will you do with that?
Mariza	What?
Teacher	My watch. You've stolen it.
	Marcelo finds the watch on Mariza and puts it back on the Teacher's wrist.
Marcelo	You've to be faster and run.
Mariza	I was going to sell it for food.
Marcelo	You can have lunch here.
Mariza	I don't like it here.
Teacher	Do you have to come here to steal?
	Mariza doesn't answer.
	No stealing here. No drugs, no smoking, no glue sniffing. No knives. These are the rules of the Centre. If you break them you'll be thrown out.
Mariza	You said I could call you Mum.
Marcelo	She's Auntie!
Teacher	I told you don't call me Auntie!
	She speaks to Mariza.
	Okay, you can call me Mum for now.
Marcelo	Mum!?

Act Two, Scene Ten

Teacher Mind your business!
Marcelo Mummy! Mummy! Mummy!
Teacher Don't mind him.

Carrot, another streetkid comes on, with a shoeshine box.

Carrot I've made a hundred cruzados! Auntie, put them in the bank for me! One more week and I'll be able to pay for the kit! I can start getting rich now!
Teacher I'm sure you will. Go in the queue for your dinner.
Carrot And tonight I'm going to sell badges and juicy gums to the tourists! And tomorrow a paper run. I'll buy myself a house before I'm ten!

Mariza speaks to the Teacher.

Mariza Would you like a house, Mum?
Teacher Ehm.
Mariza Yes. A house in town. Will it make you very happy?
Teacher A house's very expensive. Many people can't even buy it after a whole life's work.
Mariza A brick house, not a shack. We wouldn't have to walk every morning and night to the market.
Teacher To the market?
Mariza We can sell flowers in the market.
Teacher I'm a teacher.
Mariza Would you like a house, Mum?

The Teacher regrets having allowed Mariza to call her 'Mum'.

Teacher Okay, it's time for a shower now.
Mariza Yes, Mum.
Marcelo Mummy! Mummy! Mummy!

Carrot echoes jokingly.

Carrot Mummy! Mummy! Mummy!

The Teacher begins to get angry.

Teacher Shut up!

Mariza looks perplexed.
Come on, to the showers!
They follow the Teacher off.

Scene Eleven

The street. Marcelo and Mariza come on. She is with her shoeshining kit. She settles on one spot. Carrot comes on and off, each time doing a different job with great enthusiasm, paper run, selling badges, carrying crates. Marcelo notices him.

Marcelo I'm going to become rich and buy myself a bike.

Mariza And then?

Marcelo And then I'll buy myself a car.

Mariza And then?

Marcelo And then I buy myself a plane.

Mariza Don't you want a house?

Marcelo What for? Streetkids don't need a house.

Mariza For your mum?

Marcelo Who cares about mums. She was always quarrelling with my dad about money. There was no money whatsoever in the house but my parents were all the time at each other's throats about it. Isn't that stupid?

Mariza My mum is not like that. When I asked for money she always gave it to me.

Marcelo Really!?

Mariza Yes, as much money as I wanted.

Marcelo I wish my mum was like that! And you left her!?

Mariza I am a bad girl. I spent all my mum's money. She wanted it back. I ran off.

Marcelo notices Carrot again.

Marcelo To be unemployed at nine! It's not right, is it? I'm really angry!

Act Two, Scene Eleven

Mariza You can do a paper run.

Marcelo I want a proper job! They use kids for grown-up work so they pay us peanuts! I want to be paid properly or nothing! I won't be a slave! I'll get rich all right.

Mariza How will you get rich if you don't work?

Marcelo You see this?

Mariza That's Rambo's knife.

Marcelo I'll become a gang leader. I'll be the next Rambo. I found his cap as well.

He shows it, without putting it on. A Man hurries on.

Man Come on, you scum! Get going with those brushes, I've an appointment.

Mariza Why are you calling us scum?

Man Because you're dirty, you smell.

Mariza I had a shower yesterday.

Man You never had a shower in your life.

Marcelo Tha's not true! We can have showers now, in the Drop-in Centre! If you call us scum again –

Man Oh, yes, will you call the police?

Mariza No, I'll tell my mum.

Man You've got a mum, have you? In the gutter somewhere?

Mariza She's a street teacher!

Man Ah. One of those missionaries! A mother of a thousand children.

Marcelo Have you heard of Rambo, Senhor?

Man Oh, that scamp. I was glad when I read that the cops had killed him. Just what Rambo needed, a bullet in the head.

Marcelo puts on the cap and pulls out the knife.

Marcelo Well, Rambo is now back from the dead.

Man Hey, no, no. Look . . . this is the money. Wonderful job.

Mariza	I haven't started yet.
Marcelo	Don't you ever say 'scum' to a streetkid.
	The Man begins to leave.
Man	Muggers! Muggers!
Mariza	Hey, that was great! Marcelo, you won't be allowed in the Centre with the knife.
Marcelo	I don't want to. I like the street. Pass on the word, Rambo's back.
	Marcelo exits with a Rambo-walk.

Scene Twelve

The Drop-in Centre. The Teacher comes on with a chair and a primer book. Mariza comes on. The Teacher gestures her to sit down. She puts the book in Mariza's hands.

Mariza looks into the book, then closes it and repeats what is on the page to the Teacher.

Mariza A – Air. B – Beans. C – Child. F – ?

Teacher Friend.

Mariza F – Friend. L – Lemon. M – ?

Teacher M – Monster.

Mariza M –

She is going to say 'monster', but switches.

M – Mum.

There is a pause. Mariza is left looking at the Teacher. The Teacher senses her gaze.

Teacher T – Teacher.

She stresses.

I am your teacher, not your mum.

Suddenly Mariza throws away the book and gets up. The Teacher picks up the book and gives it back to her. She invites Mariza to sit down again. Suddenly Mariza throws away the book and the chair. The Teacher puts the chair back in place and gives the book back to Mariza. She invites her to sit down. Mariza throws the book at her and runs off.

Scene Thirteen

The street. Mariza comes on. She puts the battered doll, which now has the head missing, at her side and starts begging. She does this without conviction or words, just holding her hand out passively to passers-by. Mum comes on, also head bent. She starts begging on the opposite pavement. Then gradually Mum sees something familiar in the girl on the opposite pavement. But there is heavy traffic and noise between them. Dodging the traffic, her heart pounding and not believing her eyes, Mum at last makes it to the other side. As a confirmation, she notices the battered doll at Mariza's side. Mariza, head bent, only sees a shadow in front of her. Mariza begins to beg automatically.

Mariza Please, please, please.

Mum is overwhelmed.

Mum Mariza.

Mariza jumps up. The ragged woman in front of her does not conform to the image she has created of her Mum. Refusing to believe the beggar she sees there to be her Mum she runs off. Mum picks up the battered doll Mariza has left behind. She rushes off in Mariza's direction.

Scene Fourteen

The Drop-in Centre. The Teacher comes on with the chair and a book, followed by the ever enthusiastic Carrot. She invites Carrot to sit down.

Carrot	Eight by eight, sixty-four. Nine by nine, eighty-one. Seven by seven, forty-nine. Nineteen by nineteen, three-hundred-sixty-one.
Teacher	What? What did you say?

Carrot is discreetly using a calculator.

Carrot	Nineteen by nineteen, three-hundred-sixty-one. Twenty-three by twenty-three –

The Teacher interrupts.

Teacher	You're a genius. You don't need a street teacher anymore, Carrot. You should go straight to university.

Mariza runs, in, all huffing and panting.

Carrot	Will they take me? I'm only eight. How do I get into university? Tell me, Teacher.

The Teacher has sensed that the newcomer is Mariza.

Teacher	Carrot, nothing is going to stop you from making it.
Carrot	It's –

The Teacher interrupts.

Teacher	I know.

She addresses Mariza.

Get out! We don't need troublemakers here! I told you the rules here and you broke them! Out. Out this minute!

Mariza	No, Mum. Please.
Teacher	I'm not your mum! Go away! There're hundreds of kids I've to think of, not just you.
Mariza	You're lying! You are my mum! You said I could call you Mum!
Teacher	Go away!
Mariza	Liar! You're a liar!

Mum comes in, behind Mariza's back. Seeing her, Mariza starts to run away from her and hides behind the Teacher.

Teacher I've had enough of you! And you are making my work impossible with your tantrums! Out!

She speaks to Mum.

Can I help you?

Mum keeps looking for Mariza who hides behind the Teacher. She senses Mum's state.

Can I help you?

Mum Mariza.

She speaks to the Teacher.

She's my daughter.

Teacher What?

Mum looks at the bundle in her arms, then throws it away.

Mum I thought she was dead.

Teacher Your daughter?

There is a pause. Mariza suddenly speaks to the Teacher.

Mariza It's not true!

Mum looks hurt.

Mum I looked for you all over the place for a whole year.

Teacher Is she your mum?

Mariza No, she's not. My mum is well dressed. She only goes about in a car. My mum's got perfume and nice shoes and all nice things.

Teacher And her face?

Mariza Her face?

Teacher What does your mum look like?

Mariza My mum's blond, with lipstick.

Teacher Mariza, is the Senhora here your mum?

Mariza She's a witch, come to grab me!

Teacher I'm sorry, Senhora. You must leave. This is a Drop-in Centre for streetkids only. There's a church up the

	road. They might give you a sandwich and something to drink.
Mariza	She's only a beggar. A lousy beggar!
	Mariza addresses the Teacher.
	You're my mum, not her!
	The Teacher realises there's something wrong and addresses Mum.
Teacher	No, don't go yet.
	Mum cries. Slowly she gets out the doll.
Mum	This's the doll she had that night on the road, when I lost her.
Mariza	My mum wouldn't leave me on a road on my own.
Mum	I didn't leave you. I lost you. Senhorita. I left Mariza and her sister Tania a night on the road. I needed to hurry home. When I went back to look for them they were both gone. Six months ago I found her sister, Tania. She died in my arms and I thought Mariza too was dead. Then, today I saw Mariza. There, right in front, on the other pavement. Me begging here and her begging there.
Mariza	My mum would have never left me.
Teacher	The Senhora said she had to hurry home.
Mariza	She never taught me anything good like reading and writing.
Mum	I don't know myself how to read and write.
Mariza	She never taught me how to dress properly and be polite.
Teacher	How could she teach you anything? Nobody taught her anything.
Mum	I could never give much to my daughters.
Mariza	You see? She never did nothing for me.
Mum	Have I been a bad mother?
Teacher	How could you give Mariza anything, Senhora, if nobody has ever given anything to you? You were not a bad mother.

Act Two, Scene Fourteen

Mum Their father went off years ago. Never heard of him again. My life has been walking to town in the morning to sell flowers in the street. Then back to the favela at night. Every day. All for a few cruzados, to make sure my children wouldn't starve.

Teacher You have done more than many mothers would.

Mariza I am going to die. Like all the other streetkids!

Mum My children were my only reason for living. I looked for them all this time, didn't I? Tania is dead and now Mariza doesn't want me. I wish I was never born.

Mum picks up the piece of the wood and the coat and remakes the bundle before going. The Teacher addresses Mariza.

Teacher Once she's gone you may never find her again. You can call other people, many people, 'Mum' but she is the one. Nobody'll love you more than her.

Mariza She never taught me anything.

Teacher She never had a teacher.

But Mariza seems unaffected by the Teacher's plea. Then suddenly, before Mum can exit.

Mariza Mum!

Mum freezes, unable to turn. There is a pause. Slowly Mariza goes up to her mum.

Mum. You don't have to teach me. I'll teach you. I'll teach you many things. I can work, I can do many jobs at once and buy a house. No one in the world is more important than you or me.

There is a pause. Then Mariza throws herself in Mum's arms. Hand in hand, they start to leave. Mariza stops, comes back to the Teacher and picks up the primer, without opening it.

A – air. B – beans. C – child. F – ?

Teacher Friend.

Mariza pauses to think and looks at the Teacher.

Mariza F – friend.

The Teacher nods. Mariza goes back to her mum, takes her hand and they exit. Carrot and the Teacher look at them as they go.

The End.

QUESTIONS AND EXPLORATIONS

Burning Everest

1 Keeping Track

Act One: Scene One

1 What does Jim mean when he says that Everest is beautiful, but not in a 'nice, sunny day in spring' way?

2 Read carefully through Jim's long speech on Chomolungma. What do you find out about George Mallory's expedition?

3 At what point do you realise that Jim's 'expedition' exists only in his imagination?

4 Sharon is Jim's mum. What effect do her first two lines have on Jim?

Act One: Scene Two

1 What are your impressions of the Welland family? What are they like? How do they treat each other? Has Jim come from a similar background?

Act One: Scene Three

2 Despite what Matt says about Jim's mother not wanting him, Jim still defends her when Stubby says, '*She's a rotten mum to throw you out in the first place*'. Why is this?

Act One: Scene Six

1 Jim is very awkward and difficult when he meets the Wellands. Why is this?

2 What does Miranda do to try to make Jim feel welcome.

Act One: Scene Seven

1 What sort of man is the Head? What do you think of his first meeting with Jim?
2 Peter has his future very carefully planned. What sort of person do you think he is?
3 How does Jim react to Peter and Miranda? Why does he react in this way?

Act One: Scene Eight

1 Even though Jim is desperate to see his mother, she is reluctant to see him. Can you see the situation from her point of view too?

Act One: Scene Nine

1 How does Mr Cooper treat Jim? What tone of voice is he using when he says, *'It seems we've had a trendsetter join the school'*?
2 How do you think Jim feels when Mr Cooper mentions his mum?

Act One: Scene Ten

1 Jim deliberately cuts up the new sports gear that Mrs Welland has bought him. What do you think he is thinking at the time?

Act One: Scene Eleven

1 Why do you think Sharon doesn't want to be alone with Jim?

Act One: Scene Twelve

1 Imagine you are Sharon. Write a letter to Jim explaining why you've made your decision and how you feel.

Questions and Explorations

Act One: Scene Fourteen

1 Do you think Jim really thinks Miranda is 'horrible'? Why?
2 Who is the more imaginative of the two; Stubby or Jim? Find evidence to support your answer.
3 When Jim says *'somewhere that doesn't concern little girls.'* and *'There weren't any girls on the Everest expedition'*, how would you describe his attitude?

Act One: Scene Fifteen

1 Miranda, talking about Stubby says, *because of his ...* and stops herself from continuing her sentence. What was she going to say? Why doesn't she say it?
2 Miranda says *'Why do people make fun of each other?'* Try to answer this.
3 Would people laugh at Miranda because of her father? Why might he become depressed?
4 Why does Jim smash the window?

Act Two: Scene One

1 Mr Welland describes Jim as 'lucky'. Is Jim lucky? Does he feel lucky?
2 Mr Welland asks Jim: *'Do you think smashing his window's going to make him any better towards handicapped people?'* Would Jim's actions have altered Matt's attitudes? What other approach might Jim have taken?
3 Why doesn't Jim like to hear Mr Welland describe Stubby as handicapped?
4 Do you think that Sharon loves Jim?

Act Two: Scene Two

1 What does the expression '*a leopard can't change his spots*' mean? Do you agree with it in Jim's case?

Act Two: Scene Three

1 The Headmaster just does not seem to want to listen to Jim. Why not? How do his reactions to Jim's story affect Jim?

Act Two: Scene Five

1 Just when it seems as though Jim's mum is coming round, we find out one reason why Sharon is cutting herself off from him. What is it?

Act Two: Scene Six

1 Why do you think Jim escapes into his fantasy world just after he has heard his mum's news?

Act Two: Scene Seven

1 How do you think the Wellands will react to what Jim has said to the Headmaster?

Act Two: Scene Eight

1 When Jim says, '*at least I'm not mad*' how do you think Jim, Miranda and Mr Welland feel at that moment? Why does Jim say it, when he knows that he shouldn't?

Act Two: Scene Nine

1 Jim (as Mallory) says, '*I kept slogging on through this hellish gale, knowing that I'd never get any higher.*' So why does he continue?

2 Why do you think Jim calls Stubby a 'plastic man' now when he has always defended Stubby in the past?

3 Why do you think it is so important to Jim to be alone?

Act Two: Scene Ten

1 What do you think about Tony's attitude towards Jim's disappearance?

Act Two: Scene Eleven

1 Why does Miranda face this danger to reach Jim?

2 It seems as though Miranda too has problems of her own. What are they?

Act Two: Scene Twelve

1 When Jim burns the poster at the end, it is obviously a very important moment in the play (so important that it gave the play its title.) Try to explain what the significance of him burning the poster is.

2 Explorations

A Mallory's Expedition

As we watch the play, Jim gives us information about Mallory's expedition to Everest. Make notes on the facts concerning the expedition.

Read this extract by Mallory on an earlier attempt at climbing Everest.

... it may be said that one factor beyond all others is required for success. Too many changes are against the climbers; too many contingencies may turn against them. Anything like a breakdown of the transport will be fatal; soft snow on the mountain will be an impregnable defence; a big wind will send back the strongest; even so small a matter as a boot fitting a shade too tight may endanger one man's foot and involve the whole party in retreat. The climbers must have above all things, if they are to win through, good fortune – and the greatest good fortune of all for mountaineers, some constant spirit of kindness in Mount Everest itself, the forgetfulness for long enough of its more cruel moods; for we must remember that the highest of mountains is capable of severity, a severity so awful and so fatal that the wiser sort of men do well to think and tremble even on the threshold of their high endeavour.

George Mallory

(from *Everest Reconnaissance – The First Expedition of 1921* by Charles Howard-Bury and George Leigh-Mallory. Edited by Marian Keaney. Hodder & Stoughton. Page 242.)

Look back at Jim's imaginative ascents of Everest. Write down the emotions Jim was experiencing during each imaginative climb.

Why does Adrian Flynn choose to make the story of a man who tried to reach the top of Everest, such an obviously important part of a play which is really about a boy trying to get back with a mother who has rejected him?

B Hurt

In groups, discuss the cruel things that Jim says and does to the other characters in the play, especially: Miranda

Mr and Mrs Welland

Stubby

Matt

Why does he say these things?
How does he feel as he is saying them?

C Character

Mr Bryant, Mrs Pryme and Mr Cooper have different views of Jim. Mrs Pryme has more sympathy for his situation, for example.

Choose one of the people who work at St Xavier's. Imagining that you are him or her, write a report on Jim during his first month at the school.

Compare your report with a partner who has chosen a different character.

D Stereotypes

Jim is not the only character who faces difficulties in the play. In groups discuss:

What problems does Miranda's father have?
Why is Miranda so unwilling to tell people about her father's problem?
Do you think people would treat him differently if they knew about it?

Jim says of Stubby: *'Everyone knocks him because of his leg. It's not right. He can do all sorts when he wants to.'*
What difficulties does Stubby face? How do people treat him? Is this fair? What can be done about it?

E Daydreaming

At what points does Jim tend to start to daydream?
List them in order.

Does any pattern emerge?
Why does he daydream?

It's very common for children to escape real life by entering a fantasy world. For example, many young children have imaginary friends to chat to if they're feeling a bit lonely.

Using the imagination to escape from the difficulties of everyday life features in various plays and novels. Two famous examples, along a similar theme are *Billy Liar* by Keith Waterhouse and *Ernie's Incredible Illucinations* by Alan Ayckbourn.

Here is an extract from the Ayckbourn play. Ernie talks to the audience about how his daydreams seem to take over his life.

> It started with these daydreams. You know, the sort everybody gets. Where you suddenly score a hat trick in the last five mintues of the Cup Final ... or saving your granny from a blazing helicopter, all that sort of rubbish.

This extract is from *Billy Liar*.

> Lying in bed. I abandoned the facts again and was back in Ambrosia.
>
> By rights, the march-past started in the Avenue of the Presidents, but it was an easy thing to shift the whole thing into Town Square. My friends had vantage seats on the town hall steps where no flag flew more proudly than the tattered blue star of the Ambrosian Federation, the standard we had carried into battle. One by one the regiment marched past, and when they had gone – the Guards, the Parachute Regiment, the King's Own Yorkshire Light Infantry – a hush fell over the crowds and they removed their hats for the proud remnants of the Ambrosian Grand Yeomanry. It was true that we had entered the war late, and some criticised us for that: but out of two thousand who went into battle only seven remained to hear the rebuke. We limped along as we had arrived from the battlefield, the mud still on our shredded uniforms, but with a proud swing to our kilts. The band played 'March of the Movies'. The war memorial was decked with blue poppies, the strange bloom found only in Ambrosia.
>
> My mother shouted up the stairs: 'Billy? Are you getting up?' The third call in a fairly well-established series of street-cries that graduated from: 'Are you awake, Billy?' to 'It's a quarter past nine, and you can stay in bed

all day for all I care', meaning twenty to nine and time to get up. I waited until she called: 'If I come up there you'll know about it' (a variant of number five, usually 'If I come up there I shall tip you out') and then I got up.

See if you can find copies of *Billy Liar* and *Ernie's Incredible Illucinations*. They're well worth a read!

Why do you think that daydreaming is such a popular theme for writers?

Write your own short play in which someone's ordinary life is interrupted by daydreams.

GLOSSARY

revealed	shown
abates	quietens down
Chomolungma	Tibetan name for Everest
summit	top
Irvine / *Odell*	men who accompanied Mallory on his expeditions on Everest
faltering	hesitating
discreetly	with subtlety
inspired	exhalted
upheaval	change
rottie	rottweiller
releases	lets go
prosthetic	artificial
preoccupied	having your mind on something else
reproving	blaming
follows suit	to do the same as
response	answer
defiantly	refusing to obey
appropriately	suitably
pompous	snobbish, over-confident
react	respond to
ambitious	keen to do well
Oxford or Cambridge	the universities
steward	attendant
eurythmics	rhythmic body movements
insolent	rude
shredded	cut up
treacherous	extremely dangerous

Glossary

avalanche	snow falling quickly down mountainside
Linford Christie	talented British athlete
Michael Jordan	talented American basketball player
Mr Schwarzenegger	American action movie actor
indicated	showed
structure	framework
absently	not concentrating
vertigo	fear of heights
ascent	climb
downstage	towards the front of the stage
methodically	systematically, carefully
sycophantically	grovelling
Torvill and Dean	famous British skating partnership
freeze	as stage directions, this means to stand absolutely still
throttle	strangle
mortified	horrified
contemplating	considering, thinking about
vacantly	emptily
tenuous	flimsy
vertical	straight up and down

QUESTIONS AND EXPLORATIONS

Mariza's Story

1   Keeping Track

Act One: Scene One

1   Why don't the cars stop for Mariza, Tania and Mum?
2   Why are they finding this particular trip harder than usual?

Act One: Scene Two

1   What is their shack made of?
2   Why is Mum so upset at losing her shack?
3   What do you think of the thieves?

Act One: Scene Four

1   What dangers will Mariza face on her own?
2   In addition to losing her home, Mum has now lost her two daughters. Try to think of adjectives to describe how she must feel at this moment.

Act One: Scene Seven

1   Why is the policeman so unhelpful?

Act One: Scene Ten

1   Why does Mariza mistake the Old Woman for her mum?

Act One: Scene Eleven

1   Everyone seems to be so unhelpful (eg Anita, Marcelo, the Old Woman). Why is this?

Act One: Scene Twelve

1   Is the Old Woman cruel for getting Mariza to steal cake?
2   Why does Anita get shot?
    Is this fair?
3   Why does the Cop demand half of everything the Old Woman earns through begging?

Act One: Scene Fourteen

1   Look carefully at the beginning of the scene again. Who has beaten Mariza up and why?
2   Why does Rambo want Marcelo to steal the kit from Mariza?

Act One: Scene Fifteen

1   Look at how Mariza describes her mum. Is this description a fair one? Why does she say these things?

Act One: Scene Eighteen

1   How is the confusion caused over Mariza calling Anita's dad Dad?

Act One: Scene Twenty

1   When Tania is shot dead for stealing bread the man says: You should have taught your daughter not to steal. Her mother replies: How could I teach her to go hungry. Whose comment do you agree with more?

Act One: Scene Twenty-one

1 We find out who the mysterious figure really is. Why has there been such a sinister build up?

Act Two: Scene Three

1 Why are the children pretending to play football?
2 The stage directions read: They all have trouble playing with a 'real' ball. They keep missing it. . . .
   Why are they so bad at football?

Act Two: Scene Four

1 Clearly Mariza's mum is acting strangely. Why is this? Why does she say I'm much happier to have a piece of wood for a daughter than a real one?

Act Two: Scene Five

1 Rambo has been killed. Who do you think has done it?
   Think about the reaction of a) his friends and b) the shop owner.
   Is this the way you'd expect people to react at the death of a child?

Act Two: Scene Six

1 The rich children throw bits of sandwiches to Anita. Are they kind?
2 When reading aloud, how could you show the differences between the children who live in the house and the street children? (Think about how to use your voice/accent.)

Act Two: Scene Eight

1 Why does Mariza want to die?
   How does she react to the death of her friend?

Act Two: Scene Eleven

1 Mariza continues to tell stories. Why?

2 Explorations

A Staging *Mariza's Story*

1 Even though there are many characters in the play, if actors 'double up' only seven actors are needed. Why do theatre companies often 'double up' in this way?

2 How would you help an actor to create several different characters, ensuring that the audience would not become confused? Think of:
   a) simple costume changes
   b) use of voice/movement, etc.

   Remember each character must have its own individual personality and mannerisms.

3 Chose three characters that interest you. Design their costumes.

B The Set

1 In the stage directions, the playwright suggests that the set should be made up of a number of cardboard boxes. One

reason for this is to keep the cost of the production down. Can you think of other reasons why cardboard boxes would be appropriate?

2 In groups, design a set for *Mariza's Story*.

You could either use different shapes and arrangements of cardboard boxes or suggest other props. First decide what shape the stage will be and where the audience will be sitting. For example, will it be round or square? Draw the outline of the stage.

Now think about how you would simply and effectively create each of these locations:

a) the long road
b) the bakery
c) the school
d) the football pitch

You could either use different shapes and arrangements of cardboard boxes or suggest other props.

Draw a plan for your locations on your outline of the stage.

C Brazilian Street Children

Although a piece of fiction, *Mariza's Story* represents the real lives of many children. In Brazil, Colombia and other South American countries huge numbers of children live on the streets. They have to face the problems of finding food, staying warm, staying alive. Many don't survive, many end up hooked on drugs.

Despite the fact that the children are not responsible for the situation they find themselves in, some adults have no sympathy for them.

Think back to the play.

Questions and Explorations

1. How does the driver treat Tania at the beginning of the play?
2. Who says the following lines?
   a) These street kids are all thieves! As far as I'm concerned they're pests!
   b) you scum . . . you're dirty, you smell . . .
   c) Just what Rambo needed, a bullet in the head.

Moreover, these adults don't just disapprove of the children.

Anita They killed another kid.
Marcelo It's the police and the killers paid by the shop owners to get rid of kids.

Try to research this subject. There are often articles in the newspapers and TV documentaries about it. What should be done to protect these children?

D Character

1. Mariza's mother searches long and hard to find her daughters. Imagine she has produced posters to display around the city. Produce such a poster – include a sketch of Mariza, details of age, name, physical description, etc.

2. Although Mariza is eight she has spent just one year in school and cannot read or write. You are to be her scribe. Put her thoughts and ideas down on paper for her. Choose three points of the play on which you think Mariza would have plenty to say and write down her thoughts. Write in the first person (ie write I/me not she/her).

E Mothers

1. Mariza wanders the streets, at first searching for her mum. But she's young and she's tired. Soon the memory of her real

mother begins to fade and she replaces old memories with snatches of new, imagined ones. Think about the people she pretends are her parents (re-read these sections):

The Old Woman (Act One: Scene Twelve)
The Lady (Act One: Scene Fifteen)
Anita's Dad (Act One: Scene Eighteen)
The Teacher (Act Two: Scene Ten)

2 Also think about how she describes her mother to the people. In Act One: Scene Fifteen she describes her as: well dressed and beautiful . . . and she had a lot of money.

She also pretends that 'Wonderwoman on the poster is her mum. Why does she tell these lies?

GLOSSARY

location	place
massacre	slaughter
mistreatment	bad treatment
persecution	to be hunted down
imitated	copied
resume	continue
hailing	trying to attract the attention of
assesses	judges
favela	shanty town
senhor	Mr (title for a man)
hesitancy	delay in making a decision
pillage	steal and spoil
loot	steal
affliction	distress
tormented	suffering
independently	on one's own
scornfully	with contempt
skyscrapers	very tall buildings
overwhelmed	unable to cope
discarded	abandoned
intentions	purpose
stealthily	carefully
accusingly	blaming
immense	enormous
enveloped	covered
emerges	comes into view
abandon	leave
contempt	scorn

cruzado	unit of Brazilian currency
senhora	Mrs (title for a married woman)
passively	submissively
foxily	craftily
scavenging	hunting desperately for food
sinister	threatening
parasite	someone living at the expense of others
promptly	quickly
anxiety	worry
wary	nervous, unsure
enlarges	grows
dishevelled	in a mess
brandishes	waves, flourishes
perplexed	totally confused
stalks	follows, tracks
all and sundry	everyone
occurrence	happening
intonation	tone of voice
participation	taking part
withdraws	leaves
confrontation	face to face with
tentatively	carefully
improvised	made up
restraining	holding back
indistinct	sound unable to be heard
famished	extremely hungry
illusion	the appearance of
vitality	energy
pursuing	chasing
senhorita	Miss (title for an unmarried woman)
conform	to fit in with
distorted	twisted out of shape